Children's Stories in Play Therapy

of related interest

Play Therapy with Abused Children
Ann Cattanach
ISBN 1 85302 193 8

Play Therapy
Where the Sky Meets the Underworld
Ann Cattanach
ISBN 1 85302 211 X

Storymaking in Education and Therapy
Alida Gersie and Nancy King
ISBN 1 85302 519 4 hb
ISBN 1 85302 520 8 pb

Something to Draw On
Activitities and Interventions Using an Art Therapy Approach
Carol Ross
ISBN 1 85302 363 9

Child Play
Its Importance for Human Development
Peter Slade
ISBN 1 85302 246 2

Children's Stories in Play Therapy

Ann Cattanach

Jessica Kingsley Publishers
London and Bristol, Pennsylvania

Acknowledgements

Prowlpuss Text © 1994 Gina Wilson. Illustrations © 1994 David Parkins. 'My Best Pal' and 'Sick of Being Pushed Around' from *There's An Awful Lot of Weirdos In Our Neighbourhood* ©1987 Colin McNaughton. 'The Doom Merchant' from *Making Friends with Frankenstein* © 1993 Colin McNaughton. Reproduced by permission of Walker Books Ltd.

'Persephone Abducted', from *Mother Love* by Rita Dove. Copyright © 1995 by Rita Dove. Reprinted by permission of W.W. Norton & Company, Inc.

'maggie and milly and molly and may' is reprinted from *Complete Poems 1904-1962*, by E.E. Cummings, edited by George J. Firmage, by permission of W.W. Norton & Company Ltd. Copyright © 1956, 1984, 1991 by Trustees for the E.E.Cummiings Trust.

Nothing by Mick Inkpen, reproduced by permission of Hodder Children's Books. Copyright © 1995 by Mick Inkpen.

Paddy Clarke Ha Ha Ha by Roddy Doyle, reproduced by permission of Reed Books. Copyright © 1993 by Roddy Doyle.

The Island of the Day Before by Umberto Eco, reproduced by permission of Reed Books and RCS Libri & Grandi Opere, Italy.

St Suniti and The Dragon and *Feminist Fables* by Suniti Namjoshi, reproduced by permission of Little Brown, London and Spinafex Press, Australia.

Constructing and Reconstucting Childhood (1990) Edited by James A. and Prout A., reproduced by permission of Falmer Press.

Childhood (1996) by Chris Jenks, reproduced by permission of Routledge.

'Sweeney Astray' from *New Selected Poems 1996-1997* by Seamus Heaney (1990), reproduced by permission of Faber & Faber.

Dancing with Mr D by Burt Keizer. Reproduced by permission of Corgi an Imprint of Transworld Publishers Ltd. Copyright c 1996 by Burt Keizer. All rights reserved.

'A Work for Poets' from *Following a Lark* by George Mackay Brown, reproduced by permission of John Murray.

'Don't Call Alligator Long-Mouth Till You Cross River' from *Say It Again Granny* by John Agard, reproduced by permission of Random House.

A Humument by Tom Phillips, reproduced by permission of Thames & Hudson Ltd. Copyright © 1987 by Tom Phillips.

First published in the United Kingdom in 1997 by
Jessica Kingsley Publishers Ltd
116 Pentonville Road
London N1 9JB, England
and
1900 Frost Road, Suite 101
Bristol, PA 19007, U S A

Copyright © 1997 Ann Cattanach

Library of Congress Cataloging in Publication Data
A CIP catalogue record for this book is available from the Library of Congress

British Library Cataloguing in Publication Data
A CIP catalogue record for this book is available from the British Library

ISBN 1-85302-362-0

Printed and Bound in Great Britain by
Biddles Ltd., Guildford and King's Lynn

Contents

Chapter 1. The Purpose of a Story   1

Chapter 2. Stories and Narrative in Play Therapy   22

Chapter 3. Differentiating the Self in Stories   50

Chapter 4. Stories of Fear and Loathing   75

Chapter 5. Stories of Loss and Abandonment   115

Chapter 6. Stories of Heroes, Wishes and Dreams   165

Chapter 7. Other People's Stories   195

References   234

Subject Index   240

Author Index   247

The Purpose of a Story

'There was there was not. Shall we tell stories or sleep in our cots?'

'Sometimes I look at the Moon, and I imagine that those darker spots are caverns, cities, islands, and the places that shine are those where the sea catches the light of the sun like the glass of a mirror. I would like to tell the stories of their kings, their wars, and their revolutions, or of the unhappiness of lovers up there, who in the course of their nights sigh as they look down at our Earth. I would like to tell about war and friendship among the various parts of the body, the arms that do battle with the feet, and the veins that make love with the arteries, or the bones with the marrow. All the stories I would like to write persecute me. When I am in my chamber, it seems as if they are all around me, like little devils, and while one tugs at my ear, another tweaks my nose, and each says to me, 'Sir, write me, I am beautiful,'...

But the purpose of a story is to teach and please at once, and what it teaches is how to recognise the snares of the world'

Umberto Eco *'The Island of the Day Before'*

These reflections from Umberto Eco's novel *The Island of the Day Before* describe the powerful human desire to invent stories and what those stories might mean to the tellers and the listeners.

When I think of the children I have met as a therapist, what I most remember from those encounters are the stories they tell, and the way we make our relationship through the interplay of pleasure and pain as their stories unfold and we share the imaginary journey together.

'to teach and to please'

and to acknowledge together the 'snares of the world'.

These 'snares' are many and often as we begin to play, the first short story centres the themes that follow. Sally aged seven began this way:

'Once there was a man monster called Johnny and he was looking for a girl to eat.

He found a girl called Victoria who lived in London town.

But just as he was about to eat her she threw her pet tarantula Spike on his lap and he screamed and ran away.'

A story of how to deal with fear, an 'if only' story. We admired this Victoria, a girl who had learnt a trick or two and could follow through with action.

I was reminded of this traditional Armenian story. Sally liked it too.

The Crow and Her Children

When her children were old enough, Mother Crow called them all together to teach them how to care for themselves in the harsh cold world outside their nest.

'Children don't be rash or too sure of yourselves.

Watch out for human beings especially when you see one bend down and pick up a stone.'

'What should we do mother' asked one of the Crow children

'if we see one with a stone already in the hand?'

'Children' replied Mother Crow, 'if you can ask a question like that, it shows you are already very careful.

So you won't come to much harm.'

This was more like Sally's method of coping; watch and watch and watch for the stone in the hand. And here in the safety of the playing space, with the pet tarantula, Sally could imagine how to follow through watching with action. This was a new and interesting aspect of self for Sally and she liked her own ingenuity.

The Therapeutic Relationship

'Believe Him who tells his story first,
And bring him grapes to quench his thirst'

There is a very special quality to a relationship based on storytelling. There is the storyteller and the listener, and the story acts in the middle as a way to negotiate a shared meaning between the two.

In play therapy children tell stories as containers for their experiences, constructed into the fictional narration of a story. There is a playfulness in the communication, whatever the horror of the story, and an equality in the relationship.

There has to be a spark of recognition between storyteller and listener as the story unfolds. This is not a therapeutic intervention when the 'wise one' listens and interprets to the child, but an equal relationship between narrator and listener to facilitate the unfolding of the story. Together they share the drama of the story as the meaning unfolds.

The criterion for the story is that it is believable – as the old Arab storytellers defined a story – 'believe him who tells his story first'; not 'true' but believable, and the storyteller must be nurtured so the story line can flow.

Playfulness

'Kan Ma Kan – There Was, There Was Not.'

The therapist and child enter the child's world of play and storymaking together, to share the playfulness of creating a story. We play around with meanings. 'Once upon a time,' 'There was, there was not.' We can create a world, then deny it an existence, as we play and stop and play again.

We participate in this basic human instinct to play and tell stories about the play. In creating a story we explore the relationships between symbols and their orthodox meanings in order to create or express new possibilities of meaning.

Sally used the symbol of being consumed to express in story form what it felt like to be controlled by a monster. But there are monsters and monsters. The monster made pet was used by Victoria in the story to frighten the consuming monster. So the consuming monster is stopped by the pet monster controlled by the girl.

Who are the monsters and can they be controlled? There is a shift in the orthodox meaning of monsters which is developed in this story. These are important matters for Sally and aspects of the complexity of her life experience are explored in the complexity of her story.

We are playing with symbol systems, loosening the ties between sign and signified, transforming meanings by creating new and fresh symbolic relationships. This process is central to a child's own creation of their world and a way to make a satisfactory meaning out of life events even though those events are not directly described. Sally explored the nature of monsters through her storytelling, negotiating the hero's relationships with monsters in all its complexity.

Bruner (1990) considered that this method of negotiating and re-negotiating meanings by the mediation of narrative interpretation was one of the crowning achievements of human development.

Playfulness of this sort is a form of social interpretation. It helps us to consider the meaning of our lived experience and this is aided by comparing our lived experiences to the cultural myths and stories of our community. Within those myths and stories are what Bruner describes as 'traditions for locating and resolving divergent narratives'.

In her story Sally is testing a view of monsters which might be divergent from our cultural myths about monsters.

Jerome Bruner: Two Modes of Thought

'I Travelled Up This Road and I Travelled Down That'

Cognitive psychologists have suggested that narratives are the form in which we organise experience and that stories or the outline of stories guide not only our memory but also our experience of what is happening and what may happen in the future. That is, we take in fragments of information and organise them in a narrative form.

Bruner (1986) considers that there are two modes of thought which provide distinctive ways of constructing reality. He defines them as a good story and a well formed logical argument. Arguments convince one of their truth, stories of their lifelikeness. And we learn about the social world through narratives. He calls the logico-scientific form the paradigmatic mode and the story form the narrative mode.

The paradigmatic mode deals in general causes and makes use of procedures to assure verifiable reference and to test for empirical truth. Its language is regulated by requirements of consistency and non contradiction. The narrative mode leads to good stories, gripping drama, believable though not necessarily 'true' historical accounts. It deals in human or human-like intention and action and the vicissitudes and consequences that mark their course.

Narrative is built upon concern for the human condition. Stories reach sad, comic or absurd denouements while theoretical arguments are simply conclusive or inconclusive.

Sally's story is clearly not 'true' yet it is a gripping drama with intention, action and consequences.

Markus and Nurius (1986) suggested that when thinking of the 'self' we think not of *a* Self but of Possible Selves along with a Now

Self, and that Possible Selves represent individuals' ideas of what they *might* become and what they are *afraid* of becoming. This exploration of a Self and a variety of possible selves is what the child explores in play and storymaking and in the therapeutic use of these forms the child is exploring possible selves in the light of sad or fearful experiences.

The child who has seen a monstrous Other can explore a variety of Selves in relation to that Other in the safety of the story. And perhaps the Other can become another Self the child is afraid of becoming, and in play that Self can be enacted or described in a story and then discarded in the playing space.

Sometimes this 'other' is too fearful to be a person. Elmore's story was about a knife: He insisted that the story was so fearful that the violence had to be done by an object.

The Wicked Knife

A knife stabbed a witch because the knife didn't like her because her was kicking him.

'Don't kick me' said the knife.

'Yes, I am going to kick you' said the witch.

Then he said 'Shut up'.

The witch did nothing then the knife stabbed her.

The witch kicked the knife and made magic – spider magic.

So the spider came up and beat the knife and the knife stabbed a skeleton.

The End

Elmore and I talked about this story and the fact that nobody was taking responsibility for the actions of the knife and, in his story, you could only control a rampaging knife with magic, and witch's magic at that. This was the terror of his created world; nobody could stop physical hurt, the only transactions here were through violence, nothing could be negotiated in any other way, even magic didn't stop the knife stabbing.

Bruner (1986) stated that most of what people deal with in the social world could not exist but for the symbolic systems that bring the world into existence: national or local loyalty, money, memberships, promises, political parties. And our experience of the world of 'nature' is shaped by conceptions of it formed in discourse with others.

Reality for most people is constituted into two spheres: that of nature and that of human affairs, the former more likely to be structured in the paradigmatic mode of logic and science, the latter in the mode of story and narrative. The subjective reality that constitutes an individual's sense of his world is roughly divided into a natural and a human one.

Psychological reality is revealed when a distinction made in one domain-language, modes of organising human knowledge – whatever – can be shown to have a base in the psychological processes (such as perception, inference, memory, thought) that people use in negotiating their transactions with the world.

Bruner explores the idea of a new developmental theory of helping the young to appreciate the fact that many worlds are possible, that meaning and reality are created and not discovered, that negotiating is the art of constructing new meanings by which individuals can regulate their relations with each other.

He suggests that new child development theory will not locate all the sources of change within the individual, the solo child; for if we have learned anything from the passage of history through which we are now moving it is that man is a part of the culture he inherits and then recreates. The power to recreate reality, to reinvent culture, we will come to recognise, is where a theory of development must begin its discussion of mind.

Play Therapy as a Social Construction

'Once upon a Time Close to a Forest There Lived a Woodcutter and His Wife'

This power to recreate a reality is the process realised between the child and therapist when they invent and tell stories together.

A social construction view shows that ways of understanding the world are always historically and culturally relative. That a person can never gain access to an objective reality. That our knowledge of the world and our ways of understanding are not derived from the nature of the world as it really is but through daily interactions between people in the course of social life. These interactions are mediated through language. What we define as 'truth' is a product not of objective observation of the world but of the social processes and interactions in which people are constantly engaged with each other.

So the therapist and child construct a space and a relationship together where the child can develop a personal and social identity by finding stories to tell about the self and the lived world of that self. The partnership agreement between the child and therapist gives meaning to the play that happens. The stories created in this playing space may not be 'true' but often will be genuine and powerfully felt and expressed.

The child who has experienced difficult events needs this to be acknowledged, and the child's sense of self is developed in the space and in the relationship between the two – child and therapist.

The stories children tell in therapy are imaginative expressions of what it feels like to live in their real and imagined worlds, without power, confused about the intentions of those adults who are supposed to care for them. And, for our part, we also tell the stories passed down to use about 'the snares of the world'.

Listen to the woodcutter and his wife, the parents of *Hansel and Gretel*:

'I'll tell you what, husband,' said the wife,

'Tomorrow morning we will take the children out quite early into the thickest part of the forest.

We will light a fire and give each of them a piece of bread, then we will go out to work and leave them alone.

They won't be able to find their way back so we will be rid of them.'

Read about *Hop-O'-My-Thumb*:

The youngest child of the woodcutter and his wife was very sickly and weak.

When he was born he was only the size of a man's thumb so he was named Hop-O'-My-Thumb.

However very small bodies often contain very great souls and so it was in this case.

Just as Hop-O'-My-Thumb attained his seventh year a great famine came to the land and the family were starving.

One evening when the children were in bed, the woodcutter suggested to his wife that they take the children into the forest the next day and leave them all alone so they should be spared the pangs of seeing them die and of hearing their cries for food.

Listen to Johnny's story about parents. He was four. I asked the questions as he played and talked.

Once upon a time a mummy and a daddy had a baby.

One day the baby went a walk and got lost.

So who found the baby?

A lorry found the baby.

The mummy went to look for the baby but she died.

The daddy dies.

So who will look after the baby?

No one.

The baby doesn't die but lives on its own.

Daddy feels all right now.

He gets on the back of a dragon and goes to look for the baby.

The dragon finds the baby and daddy will look after the baby.

Mummy dies.

The baby goes home to daddy's house on the lorry.

But the baby dies because the dragon eats it all up.

> *What happens now?*

Yes daddy died.

The baby is eaten up.

> *Does anybody get better?*

No/Yes.

The police are coming now.

Daddy is dead in mud.

The baby stays dead.

The daddy stays dead

He is shut in the cage.

He flies in the cage on the back of the dragon and lands in mud.

> *What happens to the baby?*

The baby stays dead.

The story explores Johnny's ideas about the adults who inhabit his world. The story is mediated through the toys and objects he has found. It is a shared moment in his life which can be held in the relationship we have constructed with each other. For Johnny, his story was his intense creation.

The artist Ben Nicholson (1968) described how Alfred Wallis painted and he stated that to Wallis his paintings were never 'paintings' but *actual events*.

Nicholson considered that when his own work succeeded it was not a picture he created but a mental experience.

The agreement between child and therapist is that the child will play and the therapist will keep the space safe for play. The therapist acknowledges that the child has had life events which might need some sorting and the play will not be to talk about these experiences but to make up stories in which the characters might have had the same things happen to them as have happened to the child.

I say something like:

'I bet you the same things will have happened to the people in your stories as have happened to you.'

But at the end of the day what we will be doing together is playing, narrating what is happening in the play, and telling stories. When children tell sad stories they often want to say as a final comment:

'It's only a story'

'Kan ma Kan.' – It was, it was not.

This is the shared story of two sisters, Mary and Jane, who had been adopted. They invented the story together.

'This is an apple crumble story in apple crumble land.

This land was made by devils. Grown up devils.

The country was ruled by Princess Mary and Princess Jane.

They had no parents because they had died and they lived there on their own.

They were nice to everyone all the time.

Although the princesses were kind, because the country was made by devils, sometimes there was a lot of fighting.

The people who lived in the country were power rangers, mermaids, animals, fish and dinosaurs. Mostly there were animals there.

All the people and animals were put in a pile by the princesses and they were made into apple crumble and once they were made into apple crumble the princesses ate them all.

They ate the whole lot.

But it was too big.

And the princesses were very sick.'

This story was powerfully felt by Mary and Jane. They told it to their adoptive mother who also found it an intense expression and compression of the need and greed and hunger the girls felt about themselves and what it might mean for them to adapt to a new family. Like Goldilocks in the story of the three bears they couldn't get anything 'just right'. They felt powerful but afraid.

The sense of loss and isolation, power and control, expressed so clearly in the story, made a strong connection between the girls and their mother at a level which could not have been expressed in a paradigmatic mode.

The story stirred the beginnings of attachment between mother and children. Their mother asked for a copy of the story to keep. She said it was important to her. She knew so well what it felt like to be made into apple crumble and consumed by princesses. Their neediness was more understandable to her when it was expressed in this form and the girls could express the intensity of feelings they were experiencing in the chaos described in the story.

They had constructed a world in their narrative, not 'true' and yet an expression of their knowledge of the world and the adults they had met or who had parented them. They needed their model of the world to be acknowledged by myself as the therapist and also by their new mother because the story had no meaning unless it was communicated, not only to each other, but also to people in their social world. To love someone new when you have formerly lived in a world created by grown-up devils is no easy task.

And it was the first time they had made a story together without fighting to the metaphoric 'death'.

The Developing Self

'Very Small Bodies Often Contain Very Great Souls'

Gergen (1991, 1994) suggests that the self is not an object to be described once and for all but is taken to be a continuously changing and fluid history of relationships. The kind of person you are exists not within people but between them.

Bruner (1990) describes the self as distributed; not localised but continually spreading, changing, grouping and regrouping across a relational and social field. Shotter (1989) stated that people were not unchanging entities but owe what stability and constancy and uniqueness they may appear to have – their identity – to the stability and constancy of certain aspects of the activities, practices and procedures in which they can make their differences from those around them known and accountable. This, however, is determined by the relationship between 'I' and 'You'. The relationship is 'ours' and in performing within it I must proceed with the expectation that you will intervene in some way if I go 'wrong'.

This 'ours' relationship is present between child and therapist and we explore 'difference' in play and stories between child and therapist Sometimes we find a better outcome, sometimes we don't look for one.

This was a speaking day for Mandy, aged 8. Mandy often elected not to speak. Mandy says she wants to rule the whole world.

'There was once three people, two wrestlers and a pirate and somebody pushed them in slime.

It was a he baddie and he pushed them in because he felt like it.

He was just nasty that day.

The slime was grey and the people inside it felt scared and afraid that they might die.

But in the end they didn't die

They just crawled out very slowly and it hurt to crawl out.

But they did it because they really wanted to live.'

Her declaration was strongly felt and it belonged to her, to be shared with me. This was a 'me' and 'you' exploration of feeling but also a 'me' and 'me' story as many aspects of self emerged. To act for no particular reason, to be afraid and scared, to crawl very slowly through life but finally to want to live, a very clear choice.

Shotter also argues that if children are addressed as 'you' rather than having information reported to them they are being 'in-structed' in how *to be*. This kind of communication with one another can literally in-form one another's being, that is, help to make one another persons of this or that kind.

Vygotsky (1978) and Mead (1934) both considered that human consciousness was constituted through language in dialogues with others. They saw the young child as internalising social beliefs and values through these dialogues, which then become part of individual thought.

For Mead this process comes about through the child taking on the attitudes of others via language and role-play, and he defines the basis of cognition as a covert dialogue between the 'I' and the 'me', both of which are aspects of the self. Vygotsky sees the child as internalising the dialogues they have had with others and applying these to mental and practical problem solving. The nature of the origins of these dialogues means that they will always be culturally and socially saturated.

If the self is not an object to be described once and for all, but is considered to be the continuously changing and fluid history of relationships, then we can explore this fluidity in therapy.

'After all Hop-O'-My-Thumb had a great soul. He had many adventures some very chilling

His father was sent to prison for abandoning his children but in the end the family came back together.

They were sustained by the rewards Hop-O'-My-Thumb gained from the judicious use of his seven league boots.

Sadly the giant's' children didn't fare so well. The giant cut off their heads by mistake.'

The Social Construction of Emotions

'A Sultan lived with his Wife in his Palace but the Wife was Unhappy'

Rosaldo (1984) considers that feelings are not substances to be discovered but social practices organised by stories that we both enact and tell.

Feelings are structured by our forms of understanding. Feelings are bound up with the stories, myths and conventions of a culture which guide people on how to react in different circumstances. As a result, certain kinds of emotional expression and certain ways of understanding emotions become habitual and characteristic in a cultural group.

A feeling cannot be easily separated from 'thoughts' or from cultural and collective interpretations of appropriate behaviour.

People understand themselves, other people and their social and physical world through cultural stories or through meanings and practices which are many — and often contradictory or paradoxical.

Dunn (1993) in her study of young children's close relationships considered that from their second year children are increasingly articulate participants in discussion of their own relationships and from this age talk about feelings — their own and those of other people. And over the pre-school years they develop a clear grasp of the links between people's behaviour, and their intentions, desires and beliefs.

In her study, children communicated about feeling states over a wide variety of social functions when they attempted to reassure, to comfort, to provoke, to prohibit and to restrain. Of particular interest in the context of play therapy are her findings on pretend play (1987). She observed that pretend play not only provides children with an opportunity to explore social roles and rules of their world, but from as early as 24 months children play with feeling states. In her study, a very high proportion of conversations about feeling states (94 per cent) took place within the framework of pretend play. The themes of these sequences involved discussion and negotiation about pain, distress, sleepiness, hunger or sadness.

This demonstrates some children's ability to 'take on' a feeling state other than their own, to assign a pretend state to a pretend character, and to *share* this assignment of feeling states with another.

It was also found that even at 18 months some children were able in the context of pretend play with a supportive elder sibling to take part in a shared fantasy involving feeling states other than their own.

The Meat of the Tongue

A sultan lived with his wife in his palace, but his wife was unhappy.

The sultan's wife grew thinner each day.

In the same town live a poor man whose wife was fat and happy.

The sultan called the man to his court and asked for his secret. Very easy. I feed her the meat of the tongue.

So the sultan got the butcher to sell him all the tongues of all the animals that he slaughtered and the queen fed off these meats.

The queen was still sad so the sultan ordered the poor man to exchange wives.

Sadly the poor man's wife did not thrive in the palace.

The poor man after coming home at night would tell his new wife all the things he had seen and all the funny things that had happened and then he told her stories which made her shout with laughter.

The he would sing and play with his new wife and amuse her.

And the queen grew fat and was beautiful to look at.

She was smiling all day remembering the many things her new husband had told her.

When the sultan called her back she refused to come.

The sultan came to fetch her and found her beautiful and happy.

He asked her what had happened and she told him.

Then he understood *the meat of the tongue.*

Narrative Therapy: Finding a Useful Story

'There was once a lazy boy called Jack'

White and Epston (1989, 1990) developed a narrative approach in family therapy initially based on G. Bateson's (1972) ideas of restraints and information in cybernetic theory. Bateson stated that events take their course because they are restrained from taking alternative courses and that people can re-define their relationships against restraints (cultural assumptions, practices and beliefs) by expanding their roles and the drama they play in.

He argued that it is not possible for us to have an appreciation of objective reality and the meaning we ascribe to any event is determined and restrained by the network of premises and presuppositions that constitute our maps of the world. The interpretation of any event is determined by how it fits with known patterns of events. He called this 'part for whole coding'.

White's narrative therapy explores the construction and reconstruction of peoples' lives through a restorying process. He considered that persons organise and give meaning to their experience through the storying of experience and in the performance of these stories they express selected aspects of their lived experience. It therefore follows that stories are constitutive – shaping lives and relationships. These stories contain restraints which prevent people from noticing new information. The process of therapy helps the individual rediscover subjugated knowledge: unique, more benign, but suppressed stories which more fully encompass the experience of the individual.

He considered that stories are full of gaps which persons must fill in order for the story to be performed. These gaps recreate the lived experience and the imagination of the storymaker. With every performance people are reauthoring their lives.

When people define themselves in their stories it can be that some dominant stories are problem saturated and some of these stories re-consolidated by significant people in a person's life. Aspects of lived experience that fall outside the dominant story are defined as unique outcomes.

White, following Foucault, sees knowledge as inseparable from power. He is concerned with the wider social construction of attitudes and attributes, linking the individual not just to the family but to powerful cultural discourses which constantly define how people should behave and think.

This is mediated through language because of its power to make up reality rather than simply to represent it. White introduced the practice of externalising the problem which personifies the constraint that is binding the family.

The problem is located outside the person or relationship. It is objectified and given a name. The problem is mapped to define its influence on a person's life and relationships. In a separation of the problem from the dominant story, people are more able to identify unique outcomes. When these are identified, people can be invited to ascribe meaning to them. These outcomes can then be plotted into an alternative story or narrative.

As alternative stories become available to be performed, other previously neglected aspects of a person's experience can be expressed and circulated. Inviting people to be an audience to their own performance of these alternative stories enhances the survival of the stories.

In *Narrative Means to Therapeutic Ends*, White and Epston include material from their therapy with families. The stories of clients are told mainly through letters, certificates and documents and seem to be somewhat led by the therapists, and perhaps the focus on locating the problem invited a problem-solving approach which limits the description of feeling states.

Restorying in Play Therapy

'*I Will Next Time*'

The process of telling stories and using pretend play to invent fictions are themselves ways of objectifying and separating the problem from the person. Playing means that the child can try out new aspects of self by taking on a role and exploring a world in that role. The constant affirmation that 'it's only a story' gives the child the choice to incorporate a strategy they have played into their broader experience, or leave the idea behind in the playing space.

It is in the playing space, in pretend play, as Dunn described, that young children play and narrate stories about feeling states. Donovan (1996) describes group narrative functions in Dramatherapy and states:

> Role emerges from the imperative of narrative… When she (the therapist) is alert to the group task to expand the possibilities of narrative, she is equally alert to the group's need to expand its role repertoire to meet new narrative demands.

Lazy Jack

There was once a boy called Jack who was so lazy he had never done a day's work in his life.

His mother got very angry with him and said that he would get no more food or drink from her until he had worked for it.

Next day Jack hired himself to a farmer, did a good day's work, was paid a penny – but the fool lost it on the way home.

His mother told him that he should have put the penny in his pocket.

'I will next time' Jack said.

Next day Jack hired himself to the dairy farmer who gave him a jar of milk, so he put it in his pocket and there was hardly a drop left by the time he got home.

His mother, exasperated, said he should have carried it on his head.

'I will next time' Jack said.

Next day he went to the farmer again and got a cream cheese for the work so he put it on his head but it was a hot day and by the time he got home the cheese was dripping down his hair onto his shoulders. What a stink!

'You fool you should have held it in your hands' said his mother

'I will next time' Jack said.

Next day he went to the miller who gave him an old Tom cat for pay so Jack tried to carry him but the cat scratched him jumped out of his hands and ran home to the miller.

'You should have tied it with a string and led him home' said his mother.

'I will next time' Jack said.

Next day Jack went to work for a butcher and was given a fine fresh shoulder of mutton, but it didn't look so fresh when he had dragged it home on a piece of string though the mud and dirt and the puddles.

His mother was furious and shouted at Jack calling him all the bad names she could remember.

'But Mother' said Jack 'you tell me different every time.'

'Well then' said his mother 'carry it home whatever it is on your shoulder.'

She thought he couldn't go far wrong with that advice.

The next day Jack went to work for the cattle keeper and at the end of the day he was given a donkey.

He staggered from the market and struggled up the road with the donkey on his shoulder.

He passed the house of a rich man whose only daughter was deaf and dumb and had never laughed in her life.

The doctor told her father that if she could laugh she would be cured.

He had tried every which way to make her laugh but nothing happened.

Well that day she was sitting sadly at the widow when she saw a donkey's legs kicking in the air and poor old Jack sweating under his burden.

The sight was so funny that she laughed and laughed and called out 'Look father',

And the father was so happy that he ran outside and fetched Jack in.

Jack married the rich man's daughter and fetched his old mother to come and live with them in the rich man's fine house.

And they were all happy together.

CHAPTER 2

Stories and Narratives in Play Therapy

Once upon a time, and it wasn't in your time or my time but it was in the good old days.

What is a Story?

The Monster Story Again

There are monsters and they are living in Nowhere but they need to eat slime.

If they sit on the slime they die but if they eat it they don't die.

The monsters are very scared because the blue slime is coming to get them.

It goes all snodgy.

This is the blue one and the green one goes next to it.

In the end they die by themselves squishing in on the slime.

That is the end of them.

The monsters were just scary.

The *Monster Story Again* is told by Reeva aged 8.

A story describes a sequence of events and these events involve people in places. The plot develops when something happens which requires actions from the characters in the story. A story has a sequence because all the events happen over time. A story has characters who are experiencing the events and the plight into which they have fallen. Their plight may be the consequence of the events or the function of their character or a combination of both.

Turner, the anthropologist, defines a story (1982) as a social drama, a spontaneous unit of social process and a fact of everyone's experience in every human society. He considers that these social dramas have four phases. Breach, crisis, redress and either reintegration or recognition of schism.

Ricoeur (1981) describes a story as a sequence of actions and experiences of a certain number of characters, whether real or imaginary. These characters are represented in situations which change and to which they react. These changes in turn reveal hidden aspects of the situations and the characters giving rise to a new predicament which calls for thought or action or both. The response to this predicament brings the story to its conclusion. And so the world turns.

In Reeva's story the monsters are the characters and their plight is their need to eat slime. However, the slime is dangerous, because it is out to get the monsters and that is the problem. The danger of the slime is averted when it goes all 'snodgy' so the situation has changed and the monsters can eat the slime.

The monsters' response to their plight is to sit on the slime. But there is redress because the monsters die anyway by just squishing in the slime and that brings the story to an end.

This redress posed a problem which Reeva wanted to explore after her story had ended. Did the monsters die because they were monsters or did they die because they were contaminated by the slime or was it a bit of both? Can anybody die in slime or is that a function of monsters in slime? Why didn't the slime kill the monsters in the end? Important questions for Reeva.

She decided that the monsters died because the slime was contaminated, so she retold her story with that interpretation.

The meaning conveyed by the storyteller is what counts when a story is shared with an audience. A storyteller conveys the meaning of the story by the connectedness between people, actions, objects, place and time. And the meaning is partly expressed by the point of view of the storyteller.

In Play Therapy one of the functions of the therapist is to clarify meaning so that the child as storyteller can be empowered to express fully their point of view through the story. This clarification is usually done through questions so that the storyteller can make their own decisions about the story.

When therapists begin to work with children they often feel that a story has some great universal meaning and that their role is that of the 'wise one' who can magically define for the child what it is that they *really* mean.

This model of communication seems to me to deny the negotiation of meaning between the storyteller and the listener and insults the child's capacity to make their own meaning. If there is no negotiation about what the story might mean for the child, then the result can be an imbalance of power.

The child will assume that the therapist holds the key to meanings and the relationship will lose one of the primary purposes of storytelling, which is the sharing of a perspective embedded in the story. The therapist must remember that the story has a particular meaning within the relationship and has a particular resonance as it is told which is unique and of that moment.

What the story means today may not be the same tomorrow.

Stories Link the Exceptional to the Ordinary

Bruner (1990) states that stories achieve their meanings by explicating deviations from the ordinary in a comprehensible form. In this way a story forges links between the exceptional and the ordinary.

He considers that the viability of a culture inheres in its capacity for resolving conflicts, for exploring differences and renegotiating communal meanings.

So while a culture must contain a set of norms, it must also contain a set of interpretative procedures for rendering departure from the norms meaningful in terms of established patterns of belief. It is through narrative and narrative interpretations that this kind of meaning is achieved.

This means that stories and narratives are very important sources for the negotiation of meaning for children who have experienced problematic events or difficult family circumstances. It is a way to place events and characters into a cultural perspective.

Angela Carter makes an interesting point in her introduction to *The Virago Book of Fairy Tales* (1990) when she points out that fairy tale families are, in the main, dysfunctional units in which parents and step-parents are neglectful to the point of murder and sibling rivalry to the point of murder is the norm.

> 'A profile of the typical European fairy-tale family reads like that of a "family at risk" in a present day inner-city social worker's case-book, and the African and Asian families represented here offer evidence that even widely different types of family structures still create unforgivable crimes between human beings too close together.'

Children who come to Play Therapy often feel 'different' and ashamed about their circumstances and it is a comfort to hear other stories similar to their own but perhaps more horrible than their own.

> 'Have you got a sister?'
> 'The beggar man kissed her!'
> 'Have you got brother?'
> 'He's made of india rubber!'
> 'Have you got baby?'
> 'It's made of bread and gravy!'

And this is Cheryl's *The Fighting Mum and Dad*.

The Fighting Mum and Dad

The mum and dad are at the park.

They are fighting about everything.

Because they don't like each other.

The baby in the park wanders off

And can't find her mum and dad.

When he did find them

They were dead

And he lay down and slept with them.

The brother came and looked after the little baby.

The baby dinosaur came and they were friends

And he lay down with mum and dad.

A car came and tried to pick them up.

They were baddies in the car and they took the children away.

Mum and dad still was dead.

The baby was dead.

But not the brother

The baby dinosaur came and was friends with the baby.

The baby came alive.

The baby found the mum.

And this is a scary Scottish story

The Wee Bird

Adapted from Jimmie McPhee, Perthshire

The story's about a little girl. It was one fine day, her mother sent her for a joog of milk to the dairy. So she says, 'Can I take my skipping rope with me?'

Her mother was awful bad, says, 'No ye can't,' she says.

'But I won't spill the milk, Mummy, I promise.'

Well her mother says, 'Ye can take the skipping rope, but if ye spill the milk, I'll kill you'.

So the little girl takes the skipping rope, an on the way going, she's skipping with it, an she gits the milk an she's skipping away, coming back, the milk in the jug, an the jug falls an breaks so she looks for another jug.

So this kind old lady come along says, 'I've got jug, jist like the neighbour of the one you broke.' So she gives it to the little girl, and the little girl goes back fir more milk.

When she comes home her mummy says, 'Well did ye get the milk?'

She says, 'Yes mummy.'

She says, 'Let me see the jug,' an she looks in the jug, she says, 'This isn't my jug, This is a different jug'

She says, 'No it's no Mummy, she says 'that's the same jug as ye give me.'

She says 'My jug had a blue stripe on the top. This one has a red.'

So her mummy killed her and baked her in a pie.

But then her father comes in. He asked where the little girl was an the woman says, 'She'll likely be out playing.'

So she gives the man his dinner and when he eats half way through the pie, he sees this finger in it, an it had a little silver ring on it, an he looks at it an says, 'Why this is my daughter's ring what did ye do to her?'

She says, 'Well I told her if she broke my jug, I wad kill her, so I've killed her.'

'Now' he says, 'look at what ye've done. I've a good mind to kill you. But no! I'll let ye live.'

The two sons came in an the father told them whit had happened. So they started to cry.

But then Christmas came and this wee bird was always peeping through the widow an the boys put crumbs an things out to the window, the little bird ett it.

But then it was Christmas night, time fir to get the presents, then a voice cam doon the chimney:

'Brothers, brothers, look up, look up, look up an see what I've got.' So when the brothers looked up, she dropped down a bagful of toys and sweets.

Then she said

'Father, father, look up an see what I've got' She dropped the father a new suit an a letter an on the envelope it said, 'Don't open this letter until two hours after Christmas night.'

So she shouted

'Mother, mother, look up, look up an see what I've got,' an when the mother looked up, she dropped a stone, an hit the mother on the head. Killed her.

So when the two hours came, the father opened up the letter, an he read it, he says, 'Dear Father, this your little daughter. The spell is broken. Once I have killed my mother, I shall come back to you on New Year's Eve.

So New Year's Eve came, an they're waitin an waitin, waitin fir the daughter to come. But she didn't come, an then three minutes before midnight, a knock came on the window, They opened the window, the little bird came in says, 'I'm home father'.

The father says, 'Why' he says 'you're the little bird now!'

She says, 'I know, but if ye take my mother's ring pinkie, pinkie of the right hand I'll come back tae a girl.

So he goes away to where the mother was buried an takes the right pinkie, where the ring still wes, the same as on her. He took it an the little girl changed back from a bird into a girl.

When she took the ring she says 'My mother weren't really bad, it was jist that the devil was inside her bit now that she's gone, she'll be in Heaven.'

An she took the ring that was on her own pinkie, she put the two in a box, an they all lived happily ever after.

Terror, pain, loss, hatred, being different; these themes find many forms.

A Story or a Narrative

While there are many similarities there is a major distinction between a story and a narrative. A story is communicated intentionally, but a narrative can be embedded in a conversation or a communication between people and is not experienced as a story by the speakers and listeners.

A narrative is sequenced in time and conveys a meaning. It can be an imagined event or an everyday event which is described, but the communication between storyteller and audience is not formalised as in storytelling.

One of the joys of storytelling with children in therapy is that, as they tell their story, they have a commanding and formal position as the storyteller with the expectation that the therapist will take the formal role of audience and listen as the story unfolds. There is a sense of a ritual or a performance when a story is being told.

In Play Therapy children often indulge in narrative as they play. They comment on their actions but do not want this kind of talk to be formalised as a story. They often say 'This isn't a story Ann!'

Narrative is often embedded in general conversation.

In the session with Reeva after she told the monster story, as she was drawing she created a narrative about her family.

She said:

> There are just three of us.
>
> Daddy loves me but he doesn't like me anymore.
>
> My brother is a cry baby.
>
> My mum's colour is red because you see her coat is red.
>
> Dad is the boss but he doesn't live there anymore.
>
> He doesn't live in the family because we have to do as he says.
>
> When my family goes they just leave me at my house.
>
> He takes me home.
>
> My mum goes with my dad to fetch my brother.
>
> He changed into a big monster then he changed into another daddy.
>
> When he's a monster he just goes away.
>
> Such a naughty boy. He blowed some bubbles.
>
> He just said 'I'm not coming back again.'

These narratives about family have the illusion of reality which is what creates fiction. Sometimes the child is exploring hypotheses about the family as an explanation for the behaviour of individuals.

Reeva is using both her story and her narration to negotiate a meaning for herself which give her comfort and explanation. In both of Reeva's stories the monster and the dad just died or disappeared for no particular reason as far as the storyteller/narrator could fathom. In telling this Reeva is reconstructing her experience, but it is important to realise that the actual telling of a story or narrative is also an experience and through this experience of telling these stories we construct ourselves.

Neisser (1988) considers that we come to know ourselves through the construction of an extended self. It is the self we imagine, and dwell on from the past and onto the future. How we behave, feel and experience at any given moment grows in part out of the self we have woven together from all our past experiences and imaginings about the future.

Storymaking in Play Therapy: Narratives of Identity

When child and therapist meet and form a therapeutic alliance the therapist is helping the child construct a narrative of identity. It is important to recognise that we are not trying to fit the child's story, through our interpretations, into a preconceived theoretical frame which we have learned as therapists. A story is a formal creative act which requires a storyteller and a listener and a narrative is co-constructed through conversational transactions between the client and the therapist.

If these narratives and stories of identity are to be helpful it is important for the therapist to have an understanding of the child's world, starting with those who are responsible for the care of the child.

The Child's Social World

When I meet a child for the first time for Play Therapy, I begin by talking with the child and carers about why and how the child and I might play together.

It is very important that there is support for the child from their carers or the intervention will not be held emotionally and the child could be further defeated instead of uplifted.

> Johnny on the railroad, picking up stones,
> Along came an engine and broke Johnny's bones.
> 'O' said Johnny, 'that's not fair.'
> 'O' said the driver, 'I don't care.'

If the child is brought for therapy reluctantly by their carer, perhaps because a professional has determined the need, then there is a risk that the child will be made to suffer and so the intervention becomes distorted.

Rather like the family when the drunk parent comes home ranting and raging, terrorising the family then, as alcoholic remorse sets in, offers affection to the children as compensation for violence. So the message in this family is that to get nurture you must first be hurt and abused.

If the child is to suffer because the carer is angry about bringing him/her for therapy then the message for the child is the same: that you must be hurt to get nurture for yourself. The therapist then becomes part of this abusive pattern and extremes of 'good' and 'bad' are invested in individuals.

The acceptance of the child's carer is crucial if the child is to feel supported. Tracy's mother was angry at the first meeting but was able to say that she found it difficult to come to meet me because she was told to bring her daughter by the social worker and she hated clinics because she couldn't read.

We talked together and with Tracy about the possibility of therapy, that there was no compulsion and we must all agree that is would be helpful. Tracy's mother felt better when she had explained her position and heard that it was the family's free choice. Both mother and daughter agreed to the idea of play and we all agreed to proceed with therapy. Mrs B found parenting difficult but she did want the best for her child once she understood what might be helpful. Tracy never missed a meeting and her mother supported her as best she could and always brought her, even though she found the clinic a difficult place.

If we think of the child as a discrete person without considering the complexity of the ecological system in which he/she lives then it is possible that the therapist might want to take on the role of 'rescuer' which is not the function of a therapeutic relationship.

The Developing Child as Part of an Ecological System

Bateson's Theories

Bateson (1972) defined 'ecology' as a natural system that included humans and other life forms, sustained though information and energy exchanges. He placed the person and the symbolic world of culture within a system of interdependent relations. He defined the unit of survival as a flexible organism-in-its-environment. The mental characteristics of the system are immanent; not in some part but in the system as a whole. He viewed the mental process as involving the individual as part of a larger aggregate of interacting elements.

These interactions involve information exchanges and it is the totality of these information exchanges that make up the mental process of the system in which the individual is only a part. He defined the unit of mind as the totality of information exchanges essential to the life processes of the aggregate parts that make up the system, which includes humans as part of the larger biotic community.

Bronfenbrenner's Theories

Bronfenbrenner (1979) defined the ecology of human development as progressive mutual accommodation between the growing human being and the changing properties of the immediate settings in which the developing person lives. This development is affected by relations between these settings, and by the larger contexts in which the settings are embedded. He defines the ecological environment as a nesting arrangement of concentric structures, each contained within the next, rather like a set of Russian dolls.

These structures are the micro-, meso-, exo-, and macrosystems.

THE MICROSYSTEM

The microsystem is the pattern of activities roles and interpersonal relations experienced by the developing person within the immediate setting, for example home and school.

THE MESOSYSTEM

The mesosystem is the connections between two or more settings in which the developing person actively participates, for example the relations among home, school and local peer group for the child.

So, for example, the educational progress at school of a child in the care system could depend on the expectations of the teacher about the child as much as on the intelligence of the child.

THE EXOSYSTEM

The exosystem refers to one or more settings that do not involve the developing person as an active participant but in which events occur that influence what happens in the setting containing the developing person.

So what happens in the parent's workplace, for example, could profoundly affect the environment of the child. A parent working long hours because of fear of unemployment could mean long periods in day care for the child.

THE MACROSYSTEM

The macrosystem refers to consistencies in the form of the micro-, meso-, and exo-, systems in a given culture that could exist rather in the form of a blueprint. For example, one day nursery in the United Kingdom has a similar environment and function to another day nursery but appears different in other cultures, as if each country has a particular set of blueprints for day nurseries.

Between cultures these three levels of the ecosystem may be very different. The three levels can differ for socio-economic, ethnic, religious or other cultural factors so, for example, an economic crisis in a family with loss of employment could seriously affect the microsystem of the developing child so that perhaps the parents couldn't afford to pay for a nursery place. Or a local authority cut-back could close the day nursery and similarly change the microsytem of the child.

ECOLOGICAL TRANSITIONS

Bronfenbrenner states that an ecological transition occurs when a person's position in the ecological environment is altered as a result of a change in role, setting or both. These changes occur throughout the life span – for example, when the child goes to nursery, or the parent is made redundant. And the final transition to which there are no exceptions – dying.

These transitions involve biological changes and altered environmental circumstances so define accommodation between the organism and its surroundings, which is the primary focus of the ecology of human development.

As Keiser (1996) writes in *Dancing With Mister D*

> 'In a nursing home when a father or mother dies it's not unusual for something like a family reunion to get under way as all the children come rushing to the deathbed from all parts of the country or even the globe. Now that we're all here we might as well stick around because the doctor has said the end is coming. And that's how the idea of a wake arises.

> The motives for sitting up nights on end with the dying are often dubious. A repentant son who never visited his mother more than once a year now takes the opportunity to punish himself for his neglect by not stirring from her side for nights on end, though the poor woman is hardly there any longer in her dying body. For just as at birth we die head first.'

ECOLOGICAL RESEARCH

In ecological research the properties of the person and the ecosystems are viewed as interdependent and analysed in system terms. The basic unit of analysis is the 'dyad' – the two person system – and a relation happens whenever one person in a setting pays attention to or participates in the activities of another.

Learning and development are best facilitated when the developing person participates in progressively more complex patterns of reciprocal activity with someone with whom that person has developed a strong emotional attachment and when the balance of power gradually shifts in favour of the developing person. In this interaction it seems that if one member of the dyad undergoes developmental change the other is also likely to do so.

These ideas of ecological systems are important for the therapist who is considering whether a therapeutic intervention is appropriate and safe for the child who can be very powerless in his/her ecological environment. When the therapeutic hour is over the child returns to that system and there must be some form of containment there for the child.

The Setting and Materials for Play Therapy

The Setting

If the child and I, within the given circumstances of their life thus far, agree to play together, then we construct the relationship within agreed rules and boundaries.

The settings for therapy will vary according to the work of the Play Therapist, so I may meet a child in a therapy room, play room or a room in their home.

INITIAL MEETING

The initial meeting might be to talk with the whole family or the child and carers about their situation; then I might describe how we could play together.

If the child is in care and away from their family we may begin to play at the first session.

I suggest to the child that we might play and make up stories together because I have heard that scary, sad (whatever description is appropriate) things have happened to the child – and good things too. What if we play and make up stories to sort out some of these things? But the stories and play we do together is:

> 'Not about you but I bet you that the same things have happened to the people in the stories as have happened to you.'

I tell the child that they can choose how they play, and choose the toys, and if it's a story, I will write it in my special book. I show the child my book for writing stories. I try to find colourful books in which to write. My passion for stationery is well known and my books, pens and pencils are much admired by my clients.

PLAYING

The method of play is described in my book *Play Therapy with Abused Children* (1992). We have our special playing space which for me is a blue mat and when we – the child and myself – are sitting and playing on the mat then we can say what we want and play who we want. But no hitting or hurting; and we both can say 'No' if we don't want to play a particular role.

The reason for my 'not playing' a role' is simply that I don't want to be that person. Maybe it's too scary or stupid or boring and we say so. I use the same language that children use when they play together, so it's a play decision not a judgmental adult being pompous.

PLAYING AND NOT PLAYING

It is very important to define the playing space as a specific area in the environment so that the child can play and not-play in the same larger environment. If the whole room is the playing space then to 'not-play' means to leave the room.

Children play in spaces on the borders of everyday life, perhaps under the table, down in the den at the bottom of the garden, in a tent in the garden, in the bedroom, under the bed, up a broad tree.

Seamus Heaney (1990) writes:

> 'I would live happy
> in an ivy bush
> high in some twisted tree
> and never come out.'

I remember as a child playing upstairs in the attic in a small room with a bolt on the door so I could lock myself away and stop my sister interrupting me. (Interrupting is a euphemism for hitting me.) I made a register filled with the names of imaginary children and I was their teacher. 'Bossy boots' from the beginning as some children have remarked! I tell them I get it from *my* mother!

I also liked to hide in a very large wardrobe in another attic room because I liked the smell of the stored winter coats and the whiff of mothballs. It was rather exciting because I might get locked inside if I closed the door and I remembered the poem at school about the bride who hid in a wooden chest playing hide and seek and was never found!!!

Play can be fun and play can be dangerous but it is remembered in all its joy and fear.

Paddy Clarke, the hero, describes such a secret place in *Paddy Clarke Ha Ha Ha* by Roddy Doyle (1994)

> 'Under the table was a fort. With the six chairs tucked under it there was still plenty of room; it was better that way, more secret. I'd sit there for hours. This was the good table in the living room, the one that never got used, except at Christmas. I didn't have to bend my head. The roof of the table was just above me. I liked it like that. It made me concentrate on the floor and feet. I saw things. Balls of fluff, held together and made round by hair, floated on the lino. The lino had tiny cracks that got bigger if you pressed them. The sun was full of dust huge chunks of it. It made me want to stop breathing. But I loved watching it. It swayed like snow…I fell asleep in there; I used to. It was always cool in there, never cold, and warm when I wanted it to be. The lino was nice on my face. The air wasn't alive like outside, beyond the table; it was safe. It had a smell I liked.'

So we place the mat in a safe space in the play room and settle to play together. I sit on the mat and the child sits on the mat and between us are the toys.

The toys belong to me to be shared with the child and because they belong and have about them the sense of my care for them and the smell of the use children have made of them, they become special.

That is a very nurturing feeling for the child. The toys, though well worn, are cared for, respected by an adult, not demeaned as 'childish', and admired, so maybe such things are possible for the child as well as the toys. I always gesture a space between me and the child, with the toys in that space. This structures the playing.

Between you and me lies the space and we can people that space with objects, toys, stories and ourselves as we begin to play together. We both need that physical space between us where our stories can ebb and flow in the pain and joy of telling and hearing. Wells writes about play in *Floor Games* (1913) His imaginative ideas greatly influenced Lowenfeld and others.

> 'The jolliest indoor games for boys and girls demand a floor, and the home that has no floor upon which games may be played falls so far short of happiness…
>
> It must be no highway to other rooms, and well lit and airy.'

While Well's games are of their time, boys only, the empire rules and the racism that goes with those views, I must say I love the pictures of his islands and cities, and the toys and figures are magical. He deserves the credit for his imaginative and original ideas.

FRAMING THE PLAY

Bateson (1955) states that before engaging in imaginative play, children must establish a play 'frame' or context to let others know that what is happening is play; that it is not real. This is usually done by smiling and laughing.

When children play they learn to operate simultaneously at two levels.

At one level they are involved in their pretend roles and stories and focus on the make-believe meaning of objects and actions. At the same time they are aware of their own identities, the other players' real identities, and the real life meanings of the objects and actions used in the play.

Children in play can flow very easily from pretend roles back to their own identities then back again to their play roles with an ease which many adults lose, thinking such skill is 'childish'. We adults try to distinguish 'reality' from 'fantasy' in a very crude way, not really understanding that two levels of awareness of roles can operate in very sophisticated ways.

Perhaps only actors maintain this skill and understanding.

It must seem very strange to the child if an adult tries to unpick 'reality' from 'fantasy' as though they can separate them, rather in the way that we assume cognitive processes can be separated from emotional processes without any interweaving.

And when we have separated the two what do we find? Paddy Clarke knows that under the table is under the table but it is also a fort and perhaps the idea of the fort is more real and has more meaning for Paddy than the table as the table. But both co-exist at the same time.

Play Materials for Storymaking

Playing to be Creative

The toys and objects that inhabit that 'space between' support the child's creativity in play. There are three aspects of creative play which are defined as the developmental play paradigm. These three play processes are called embodiment or sensory play, projective play and enactment or role play.

EMBODIED PLAY

Embodied play is the play of small children as they expand their environment through sensory exploration. It is the way the child discovers where their body ends and the rest of the world begins.

This kind of touching, sniffing and smelling is apt to infuriate adults but is one of the great thrills of childhood. Paddy Clarke tells of such delights when he describes his hot water bottle:

'My hot water bottle was red, Manchester United's colour. Sinbad's was green. I loved the smell off the bottle. I put hot water in it and emptied it and smelled it; I put my nose to the hole, nearly in it. Lovely. You didn't just fill it with water – my ma showed me; you had to lie the bottle on its side and slowly pour the water in or else air got trapped and the rubber rotted and burst. I jumped on Sinbad's bottle. Nothing happened. I didn't do it again. Sometimes when nothing happened it was really getting ready to happen.'

Children who come from environments where they are hurt or neglected have often shut down on these sensory explorations really as a matter of survival. If you are being hit or touched in frightening ways then the safest way to cope is not to feel what is happening.

This means that some children will have poor body awareness for touch and taste. However, these children may need to be hyper vigilant, so sight and hearing can be very sophisticated because watching what the adults are doing and listening for their approach could have been a matter of life or death. You need to watch out to survive!

> Hitty pitty within the wall,
> And hitty pitty without the wall
> If you touch hitty my toy
> Hitty pitty will bite the boy.

And the trick is to keep moving.

> Anna Elsie, she jumped with surprise;
> The surprise was so quick, it played her a trick;
> The trick was so rare, she jumped in a chair;
> The chair was so frail, she jumped in a pail;
> The pail was so wet, she jumped in a net;
> The net was so small, she jumped on the ball;
> The ball was so round, she jumped on the ground;
> And ever since then she's been turning around.

So when the child is safe enough and comes to therapy there is a need to explore their environment through the senses, discovering the relationship of their embodied self to the rest of the space around them.

In the safety of the playing space that exploration, hopefully, can be enjoyed rather than experienced though fear. Watching skills learnt through terror can be re-framed in an observation game. I often play the *Change Three Things Game*.

- Sit facing each other.
- Look at your partner, visualising their appearance and how they are sitting.
- Close your eyes.
- Hold the image.
- Your partner changes three things about her appearance. (Like moving a watch to the other wrist or undoing a shoelace.)
- When your partner is ready you open your eyes.
- Guess the three things your partner has changed.
- Swap roles.

I never win.

This is also a good game for staring at someone without getting into trouble. Children want to stare at you but are usually too polite. In this game staring is allowed.

Be prepared for very personal remarks after the staring, usually about the most sensitive aspect of body care. Remarks about teeth, nails and hair are the most common – or in my case being fat!

The materials for sensory play are usually determined by place and availability. Sand and water, bubbles, play-doh and, in my play space, megaslime and especially 'gak' which is colourful, runny and messy but controllable slimy material.

The function of embodied play is to allow the child a sensory exploration of the materials without any other purpose. This in itself is a relief for most children who come with the expectation that adults want to see results similar to the attainment levels expected at school.

If you want Victorian values read *The Victorian Child's Guide to Knowledge* (Umphelby 1828).

QUESTION: What is the World?

ANSWER: The earth we live on.

QUESTION: Who made it?

ANSWER: The great and good God.

QUESTION: Are there not many things in it you would like to know about?

ANSWER: Yes, very much.

QUESTION: Pray then, what is bread made of?

ANSWER: Flour

QUESTION: What is flour?

ANSWER: Wheat ground to flour by the miller.

QUESTION: What injury is wheat liable to?

ANSWER: To three kinds of diseases, called blight, mildew, and smut.'

And so on to the end of the book! You will have to research 'smut' for yourself!

Fortunately, slime does not lend itself to purposeful use, so we can just enjoy the dripping and touching and the rather sweaty smell of the material touched by many sticky fingers. The child often uses the gak as a body fluid; for example, hanging a long piece from the nose or mouth, often as a way of trying to control the body and what comes out of the body. Also the delight in being a little outrageous to explore the shock value.

Children seem to have changed little in this respect, as I read in John Russell's *Book of Nurture* written about 1460. He advises a child working in the great lord's pantry as follows:

'Do not claw your head or your back as if you were after a flea, or stroke your hair as if you sought a louse.

…and keep your eyes free from winking and watering.

Do not pick your nose or let it drop clear pearls, or sniff or blow too loud, lest your lord hear.

Twist not your neck askew like a jackdaw; wring not your hand with picking or trifling or shrugging, as if ye would saw (wood); nor puff up your chest, not pick your ears, nor be slow of hearing

…Beware of making faces and scorning; and be no liar with your mouth. Nor yet lick your lips nor drivel.'

Sounds familiar to me!

PROJECTIVE PLAY

Children often move from sensory play to projective play with toys and other objects, developing stories by placing play figures in the messy materials.

So slime and 'gak' are often placed in little piles to become islands or space planets or just 'mess' inhabited by 'monsters' or waiting as a trap to ensnare unwary children.

Therapy is a three way channel and reflects the child, the therapist and the chosen materials. So, as slime is important in my array of play materials, many children who play with me begin storymaking with the theme of slime. Some examples:

'Once upon a time there was a monster who lives in slime'…

'The baby is drowning in slime.'…

'The ghost mask was covered in white slime'…

'I am the mightiest warrior' said the dinosaur as he jumped into the slime'…

Robert Louis Stevenson (1881) describes this process as he and his cousin played with porridge at breakfast:

'When my cousin and I took our porridge of a morning, we had a device to enliven the course of the meal. He ate his with sugar, and explained it to be a country continually buried under snow. I took mine with milk, and explained it to be a country suffering gradual inundation. You can imagine us exchanging bulletins: how here was an island still unsubmerged, here a valley not yet covered with snow; what inventions were made; how his population lived in cabins on perches and travelled on stilts, and how mine were always in boats; how the interest grew furious, as the last corner of safe ground was cut off on all sides and grew smaller every moment; and how, in fine, the food was of altogether secondary importance, and might even have been nauseous, so long as we seasoned it with these dreams.'

This movement from sensory play to projective play, integrating tactile materials with small figures and objects is the most common way a child begins storytelling. The tactile materials become a place or environment like the porridge became islands in Stevenson's description. The play figures become the characters, enter the created environment and then something happens to the characters and so a story begins. The skill of the therapist is to see the beginnings of that process and encourage its development.

This is the first story of John, aged 8, who was fostered for 4 years, then went to an adoptive placement where he was physically abused, so then returned to his original foster family. He began to play with slime and enjoyed stretching and sniffing and touching it. Then he selected a plastic crocodile with a large mouth. I asked him what the monster was called and he said 'Gaudi'. John stuffed 'gak' into Gaudi's mouth. I asked why Gaudi was eating the slime. John began this story.

'There was once a monster called Gaudi and he ate slime because he had an appetite on slime.

He ate so much purple slime that it came out of his tongue, his mouth and his brain.

(John showed me this dripping slime in the mouth of the monster as he narrated his story.)

And he was sent away to a country where people were hit and burnt and he was very scared so he ran away back to the slime country where he felt safe'.

After the story we talked about the monster and how powerless he was but he did take action for himself and ended up back in the safe place.

The toys and small objects I collect to facilitate the telling of stories are what children tell me that they like and are also from categories of heroes, villains, family groups and magical people, wild animals and farm animals, mythical creatures and pre-historic creatures, earth bound creatures and sea creatures, including mermaids.

I have two large bags containing those which seem to be the ones most used by the children as well as crocodile monsters and strange humanoids which can drip slime through the mouth and eyes. These creatures live with the slime.

MYTHICAL CREATURES AND HUMAN FIGURES

This large mixed bag of mythical creatures and humans is the bag most often chosen for storymaking. Popular figures at present include:

- The Power Rangers
- Wrestlers, pirates, Robin Hood figures, and knights
- Jurassic Park human figures male and female and dinosaurs and a small cage for dinosaurs
- A very large Tyrannosaurus Rex
- Dogs, sheep, a bull, cows
- A tiger, a bear
- Dolphins, a shark, an octopus
- Mermaids
- A large dragon

- Family figures, parents, grandparents, children
- A rather large crawling baby bigger that the other family figures
- Cars, including a police car, a rubbish truck and a small van to carry passengers
- There are trees, fences, bridges and other objects to make environments.

All the toys can be placed in sand without too much harm although the large walking baby has ceased to walk through sand damage in the joints! The toys and objects change continually as a particular child asks for some special figure or a new set of characters become popular. It is very important to listen to what the child says about the toys, as they are the experts.

Although some of these toys have a particular history on TV or film, the children do not carry this history over into storymaking in any rigid way.

Power Rangers certainly 'morph' to use magical powers but they tell different stories when used by the children. In fact Power Rangers are sometimes used as Baddies as they often look rather gruesome. This is a story using these toys.

> 'In the mermaid world lived three mermaids and a giant rat who wanted to kill the mermaids.
>
> They were scared of the rat and hid behind their leader called Ariel.
>
> The rat was angry and was specially angry with Ariel.
>
> They had some friends who was fiercer than the rat.
>
> They were the dragon and the sea monster who protected them.
>
> In the end the dragon and the dinosaur saved the mermaids and the rat died of fright'.

FAMILY DOLLS

This is a large collection of family dolls and domestic animals and small pieces of furniture. The dolls are from a variety of ethnic groups and enough for a child to describe journeys to and from six or seven families.

- About sixty small family figures, including a lot of babies
- Washing facilities, baths, potties, lavatories
- Witch's fingers for those mythical creatures who terrorise family members. (Placed there by several children.)
- Lots of toy suitcases for journeys
- Prams for the babies
- A large car for journeys.

Children usually set these dolls in family environments with the furniture and other objects and tell their stories as they move the dolls around the house or from one house to another or to the seaside for a trip.

This is a story using family dolls by Janet, aged 8, settling into her adoptive family but still finding it strange. A boy who was fostered has just left the family.

The Cosworth Family

In this family there was a dog called Peter.

The Cosworth family were moving house, because their old house had been burnt down.

But luckily they had just come back from holiday and had all their things with them so nothing got burnt.

They didn't mind about the old house because they were going to move house anyway.

Everybody is going to the new house.

At last they get there.

They like the new house.

It is small but they still liked it.

The lorry came up with all their furniture.

The baby started to cry because of the loud noise the lorry made.

The family set up their furniture in their new house.

The baby is trying to sleep.

The rest of the family are trying to set up the furniture.

They bring the suitcases in and begin to unpack.

Naughty Johnny has hidden one of the suitcases.

There are only two and there should be three.

Everybody gets fed up and they have a little rest.

The baby stops crying and goes to sleep.

The next day poor Johnny was ill and the nurse came.

The nurse gave him an injection then she went home.

The next day the doctor came.

He said that Johnny was better but he had to stay in bed for two days.

At last Johnny was better and was able to go to school again.

He had loads of friends and sometimes was naughty but only a little bit.

When Johnny grew up he got married.

He was naughty and ended up in jail for stealing from a shop.

All the children grew up, got married.

But only Johnny, the naughty boy ended up in jail.

The End

CHAPTER 3

Who Am I and Who Are You? Differentiating the Self

'The Other is what allows me not to repeat myself forever.'
Baudrillard

The Mirror

There was once a Japanese farmer who bought his young wife a mirror. She was surprised and delighted to know that the mirror reflected her face and she loved her mirror above all her possessions.

She gave birth to a daughter but sadly she died young.

The farmer put her mirror away in an old chest where it lay for many years.

The daughter grew up to be the image of her mother, and one day when she was almost a woman, her father took her aside and told her about her mother, and the mirror which she had loved so much. The girl was curious and searched the house to find the mirror.

She found the mirror in the old chest and looked into it.

'Father' she cried. 'Look, here is my mother's face.'

It was her own face she saw but her father said nothing.

The tears were streaming down his face and no words would come.

The child comes to play in therapy to construct a world which can contain their self and what might be termed 'the other' that is the rest of their world, both people and objects. But if their world has contained loss or fear or terror, it is, like it was for the girl in the story, difficult to know where you end and 'the other' begins.

The girl in *The Mirror* story has lost her mother. Her father has been unable to talk about this loss. Finally her father speaks to her and *she* has to find her mother's most treasured possession, hidden, the secret in the family.

When she looks at the reflection, she loses herself, and only sees the secret one, the lost one, the one she can never be, the unattainable one.

So where does it end? Who is this daughter? Does she have to be her lost mother or does she have a right to find her own self?

Who is the Self and Who is the Other?

Baudrillard the French post-modern writer explores ideas of the other in his book of essays *The Transparency of Evil* (1993). He explores his ideas of the other, the persons, the objects, the forms, the cultures which are 'not me':

> 'Just as what we deem fatal in catastrophes is the world's sovereign indifference to us, so what we deem fatal in seduction is the Other's sovereign otherness with respect to us.
>
> That otherness which erupts into out life, with stunning clarity, in the shape of a gesture, a face, a form, a word, a prophetic dream, a witticism, an object, a woman, or a desert.' (p.174)

The child comes to therapy trying to make some meaning of encounters with that sovereign indifference from the other, often to their very existence as a separate being. They have disturbing images of 'the other' – the loved and hated one, the safe place and the scary place, and they need another place and an emotional space to explore these paradoxes.

They come to play and make stories with the sense that they are what their abuser or tormentor tells them they are, and sometimes even that limited sense of self is so intertwined with the abusing other as to make the two of them inseparable. So for the child there is a feeling that 'I am the other and the other is me'. Or sometimes that lack of attachment creates an idealised view of the unattainable 'other' who is so unreliable that they can never be contained and held.

Jim's mother, trapped in a cycle of crime and prostitution to get crack cocaine, tries to stop, fails, tries to see her son, doesn't get there, is ill, in jail, lost, on drugs but never there for Jim. He can never express his fear and anger because she is so unattainable and when you prepare to say something she isn't there. His pain is palpable. He spends his life thinking of her. He is her slave, as Leonard Cohen sings: 'dancing to the end of love'. Their relationship has to be disentangled but at the same time the two are intertwined.

> '*And all the little monsters said in a chorus: You must kiss us*
>
> What! you who are evil,
> Ugly and uncivil.
> You who are cruel,
> Afraid and needy,
> Uncouth and seedy.
>
> *Yes, moody and greedy,*
> *Yes. You must bless us.*
>
> But the evil you do.
> The endless ado.
> Why bless you?
> You are composed of such shameful stuff.

Because said the monsters beginning to laugh,
Because they said cheering up.
You might as well. You are part of us.

The Ubiquitous Lout, in *St. Suniti and The Dragon*
(Namjoshi 1994)

So often the child who has been hurt and abused feels that *he* is the monster, *he* is the bad one, it's all *his* fault.

Jim thinks his mother doesn't come to meet him because he is not worth anything. We read the story *of Prowlpuss* together. This is a story about a rough cat:

'He's not a
sit-by-the-fire-
and purr cat,
A look-at-my-
exquisite-fur-cat,
No, he's not!

He's rough and
gruff and very
very tough.'

Prowlpuss is in love with a beautiful white cat

'High in a tree
at the alley's end,
Right at the top
so no one
can get her
or pet her
Lives one little cat
A tiny-white-star cat.
A twinkle afar cat.'

Prowlpuss lives with nice old Nellie Smith who give him unconditional love but nothing can erase his passion for the star cat.

Jim knows that passion, he imagines himself as the rough and unlovable Prowlpuss; his mother becomes this wonderful star creature. The mirror is distorted, the story twisted, the blame goes back to the child, because if you blame the star creature she will disappear. It's very very tricky.

Read the story of the crocodile:

The Crocodile

One day when the one-eyed monkey was perched on her tree, a man came along (he was carrying an axe) and asked for some plums. The monkey didn't like him but was willing to be helpful so she said 'The plums are still green, but if you come back on Monday, I will give you some.' 'Nonsense' said the man, 'of course they are ripe' and shook the tree with considerable force. No plums fell (they really were green) so the man got mad and began throwing stones. The monkey was frightened. She had already lost an eye and stones could do damage. 'Watch out' she shouted, 'there's a crocodile behind you.' 'Liar' yelled the man and threw his axe. The monkey dodged and somehow caught the axe. At the same instant the crocodile's jaws snapped up the man. When the crocodile had finished, the monkey asked how the crocodile felt. 'Full' said the crocodile, 'No' said the monkey 'what I meant is how do you feel about the moral aspect?' 'Well' said the crocodile, 'I saved your life, though it is true that you caught the axe.' 'But you killed a man,' said the monkey severely. 'All right have it your own way,' said the crocodile contentedly, 'You threw the axe. See how it sounds. 'Monkey kills Man in Sheer Self Defence.' 'No,' said the monkey, 'I didn't throw the axe,' 'True.' said the crocodile, 'You warned the man. If he had believed you, I might be dead,' 'I'm sorry' said the monkey. 'Yes' said the crocodile, 'The man was a bully. You were a victim. And I was heroic. I come out best.'

Feminist Fables Namjoshi, S.

So this is one of the explorations for the child, who is who in their world. Who is the bully, who is the hero and who is the victim? Who is to blame and who come out best? And most of all, do I now exist at all?

Look back to the girl searching for the mirror. Does the other mirror me or do I mirror the other?

Jane was 14 when she wrote this story. She had come into care when she was 4 years old. He strongest memory is going to Macdonalds for a hamburger with her social worker and never going home again. Six moves later she is living contentedly with her present carers and soon she will have been with them longer than any of her other placements. But can you trust people and who cares anyway!

Jane wrote:

Mr Nobody

'This is Mr Nobody.

He has no name and he is green.

He lives in London.

He lives with 60 other nobodies in flats which are made for nobodies.

They sit down watching TV all day.

Nobodies eat anything but especially pickled onions because they are smelly and make your breath smell.

Mr Nobody's friends look weird.

They have blue hair, eat pickled onions and scream a lot.'

So how can Jane become the somebody she wants to be, eat what she wants to eat and live as a somebody rather than a nobody?

Jane and I began by playing together. Recreate the past with baby play. The great game of peek-a-boo. Eyes closed, hands in front of the face, hiding, seeking, finding with a great shout of 'Boo!' Forever searching for the other, who comes then vanishes at my will. Or is it the other way round; when I put my hands over my face, do I vanish and the other stays? Do I have the power to make myself vanish or do I have the power to make the other vanish? Who goes and who stays?

We remembered the Cheshire cat who slowly disappears, leaving only his grin: no teeth, no mouth just a grin. Grin and bear it. Was that how it had to be? Or the Kilkenny cats who raged and devoured each other leaving behind no more that their tails. What had happened to those left behind?

Would Jane have been devoured if she had stayed with her mother? Jane thinks that would have happened. And now in the 'sort of' safety of her new home she can venture out of the safe place to dare to see her father just for a while, and not be afraid. The pain of the past was difficult to untangle.

Jane could only explore this confusion in her imaginative stories and in those stories she began to disentangle who she is from all those 'Mr Nobody' messages she heard as she grew up. And begin to think of that terrible 'other' who took her away from her family with a trick.

So who are the 'goodies' and who the 'baddies'? Was the social worker 'good' to take her from her violent family, or 'bad' because of the way she left?

> 'All the objects, places and faces that are so much a part of us that they intensify our loneliness and we are forced to love them because there will be no others after them. They have involuted into us and we into them, they have created around us the optical illusion of everyday life. At most they are capable, like a mirror, of inverting the symmetry of our lives.' (Baudrillard 1990, p.26)

What was it like to be Jane's dad, and what was it like to be the social worker?

Jane had her own ideas as she charted her life through her stories. No final conclusions, a little more tolerance of the pain and a little more hope that she is wanted by her new family. Who knows what might happen. Therapy can't control the future.

Mead (1934) emphasises the importance of this kind of role exploration for the child and states:

> 'The child during the period of infancy creates a forum within which he assumes various roles and the child's self is gradually integrated out of these socially different attitudes, always retaining the capacity of addressing itself and responding to that address with a reaction that belongs in a certain sense to another.' (p.366)

And the therapist is the listener, the other, who hears all the stories and narratives, asks questions about characters and plot and records the story because it is important and the storyteller is important. The ideas flow from storyteller to listener, because the storyteller needs their story to be validated in the mirror which is the face of the listener.

At first, the child assumes subjectively that the other, the therapist, thinks as he/she does; then, as the therapist asks questions, makes suggestions, the child discovers that ideas are not always shared and finally the therapist becomes a really other other.

This is an old Chinese story about mirrors.

The Yellow Emperor

In the legendary times of the Yellow Emperor the world of mirrors and the world of men were not as they are now, cut off from each other.

They were quite different, neither beings, nor colours nor shapes were the same.

Both kingdoms the specular and the human, lived in harmony; you could come and go through mirrors.

One night the mirror people invaded the earth. Their powers were great but the magic arts of the Yellow Emperor prevailed.

He repulsed the invaders, imprisoned them in their mirrors, and forced on them the task of repeating, as though in a kind of dream, all the actions of men.

He stripped them of their power, and of their forms and reduced them to mere slavish reflections.

But a day will come when the magic spell will be broken and the mirror creatures and the creatures of water will join together.

And then watch out!!!

So the mirroring in the relationship between child and therapist is complex.

Baudrillard (1993) defines this relationship with the other as 'subtlety' whereby we live not on our own energy or according to our own will but rather thanks to the energy and the will that we subtly spirit away from others, from the world, from those whom we love and those whom we hate. And he defines the relationship of child to adult as a strategy adapted by children: whereas adults make children believe that they, the adults, are adults, children for their part let adults believe that they, the children, are children.

Of the two strategies the second is the subtler, for while adults believe they are adults, children do not believe that they are children. They *are* children but they do not believe it.

So within that complexity of roles we explore extremities of the complexity. Extremities of the other, of murderous others, of seducers of children, of monsters who can also be loving fathers and mothers, flirtatious friends.

Sometimes the other is horror and the horror is real.

'On the one hand the other is always already dead, on the other hand the other is indestructible.' (Baudrillard 1993)

I remember watching the serial of *Pride and Prejudice* on TV and the scene where D'Arcy arrives at his mansion, hot and weary. He leaps into the lake, emerging from the water a young and exquisite creature, born to be loved.

His warmth and sexuality are all encapsulated in the visual frame of the film. Behind this vision, a view of the great house.

I had read an article the previous day which stated that rooms in the house had at one stage been repaired by Frederick West, the serial killer and abuser of children and women. The juxtaposition of the two images, Mr D'Arcy and Frederick West, seemed a defining moment. I thought of the contamination which abuse brings to the lives of those who are hurt and of those who endeavour to help them. What is left is infinite sadness, never again to admire beauty and passion without the dark images of violations of beauty and passion.

Love and Cruelty: Messing with Monsters

And all the little monsters said in a chorus
You must kiss us.

What you who are evil,
Ugly and uncivil…

You might as well. You are part of us.

This poem appears in the story of *Saint Suniti and the Dragon*.

Suniti was horrified at the thought of kissing the monsters but she dared, stretched out her hand and Grendel, the monster, grabbed it and bit her finger.

'And Suniti? Suniti just stood there, startled that for once the ready response, the well-known surge of contempt and anger, had not invaded her.

Back in her study she wrote on a clean sheet of paper:

Love is the Law,

  And Cruelty the Climate,

    Let the Cultures collide.

Then, neatly and methodically, she bandaged her finger.'

That story reminds me so much of myself the therapist 'messing with monsters.' It's a frightening business. When the cultures of love and cruelty collide we are in a dangerous space, a messy space. Into this therapeutic space comes the client, a child, telling of cruelty, and the child brings the monster other with him/her and both child and therapist have to mess with monsters in the therapeutic space.

In this process it is hard for the child to separate love and cruelty, herself from the monster who has hurt and been cruel to her, to sort out why she loves the monster who groomed her for abuse, and explore the monster inside herself who belongs to her and does not belong to the monster who abused. Some clients come to the space already defined as monsters; the learnt behaviour from the abuser labelled as their own monstrous nature. Self and other totally merged and unseparated.

The Law of Love and the Climate of Cruelty collide in the therapeutic space and the space is corrupted with the cruelty. Knowledge of such cruelty brings loss of innocence to both child and therapist.

In this context perhaps 'innocence' is not the appropriate word.

Kitzinger (1990) considers that using the concept of innocence to incite public revulsion against sexual abuse is problematic for three reasons. First, the idea of childhood innocence is itself a source of sexual excitement for abusers. Second, if 'innocence' is the ideal of childhood then it stigmatises the 'knowing' child who does not conform to the ideal. (We all know of judges who condemn 'flirtatious' children who somehow 'deserve' to be abused.) The third and most fundamental reason is that this ideology is used to deny children access to knowledge and power and hence increase their vulnerability to abuse.

These twin concepts of innocence and ignorance are vehicles for adults' double standards: a child is ignorant if she doesn't know what the adults wants her to know, but innocent if she doesn't know what adults don't want her to know. So the child has to live with her own particular experience of cruelty and the therapist has to live with the stories of many acts of cruelties, and in both cases how can we hold and frame that knowledge. The 'other' can contaminate and it is hard to disentangle.

Defining Children

One of the notions to disentangle in this complexity is the therapists' understanding of the meaning of childhood. There are many perspectives to explore when considering our ideas of childhood and these perspectives are determined by the focus of out own particular interests.

> 'Any potential theorist of childhood who wishes to engage in such an analysis,…should realise that they too are responsible for constituting the child, and that different images and representations of the child are occasioned by the different theoretical social worlds that we inhabit. In this way the passage of our theorising will continue to emerge from the sytenosis of the dominant 'natural' archetypes of childhood, being those of either the pathological or the schismatic. We need no longer abandon the child either to ignorance and secondary status or to radical difference and a bipartite world'. (Jenks 1996, p.29)

The Social Constructions of British Childhood

Hendrick (1990) delineated a variety of constructions of children through an exploration of dominant discourses about children in particular contexts from 1800 to the present. The constructions which emerged are, in chronological order, the Romantic Child, the Evangelical Child, the Factory Child, the Delinquent Child, the Schooled Child, the Psycho-medical Child, and the Welfare Child. Then two further reconstructions: from 1914 to the late 1950s the Psychological Child, and the Family Child and the Public (child in a care system) Child.

It is important to consider the diversity of experiences of childhood rather than assuming that western constructions of childhood are somehow universal.

Boyden (1990) states that there exists a core ideology in the south, (developing countries) around which official versions of childhood pivot. This ideology dictates that children are demarcated from adults by a series of biological and psychological as opposed to social, characteristics that are universally valid. The consequences of applying global standards for childhood based on western concepts of welfare may not always be helpful or meet the needs of children in developing countries.

My perspective as a therapist is to consider that children are first and foremost people at a particular developmental stage in their life span who need love, protection and security to grow healthily. But western society still perceives the child as object and adults own this object as of right. This seems particularly true of the child in care, shunted from pillar to post in an endless search for parenting, home and some sort of family.

Children are defined by their 'otherness' and we still split children into categories such as 'innocent angels' pure and vulnerable, or 'uncivilised monsters' who need to be controlled. The polarities expressed in these concepts define childhood as some exotic otherness inhabited by 'angels' and 'devils'. Many of these images emerge from Victorian literature.

Read the child as monster:

Falsehood Corrected

When Jacky drown'd our poor cat Tib,
He told a very naughty fib,
And said he had not drown'd her;
But truth is always soon found out –
No one but Jack had been about
The place where Thomas found her.

And Thomas saw him with the cat,
(Though Jacky did not know of that,)
And told Papa the trick;
He saw him take a slender string,
And round poor Pussy's neck then swing
A very heavy brick.

His parents, being very sad
To find they had a boy so bad
To say what was not true,
Determined to correct him then;
And never was he known again
Such naughty things to do.

The parents here seem more concerned about the lying than the cruelty!

Now the child as angel.

The Good Boy

When Philip's good Mamma was ill,
The servant begged he would be still;
Because the doctor and the nurse
Had said that noise would make her worse.

At night, when Philip went to bed,
He kissed Mamma, and whispering said,
'My dear Mamma, I never will
Make any noise when you are ill.'

Being good means don't annoy the adults! And this is what happens if you leave the safety of home!

The Chimney Sweep

'Sweep! sweep! sweep! sweep!' cries little Jack,
With brush and bag upon his back,
And black from head to foot;
'Sweep! sweep! sweep! sweep!' is all his song
Beneath his load of soot.

But then he was not always black,
Oh, no! he once was pretty Jack,
And had a kind papa;
But, silly child! he ran to play

Too far from home, a long, long way,
And did not ask Mamma.

So he was lost, and now must creep
Up chimneys, crying, Sweep! sweep! sweep!

These images of 'good', 'bad' and 'lost' children still persist and attract abusers who wish to corrupt and destroy as a way to achieve control over what they feel was never theirs, this vision of childhood. The 'otherness' of childhood becomes exotic and the exotic becomes erotic.

'She touched my leg' says the adult abuser justifying the abuse of a four-year-old child, 'So she made the first sexual advances'.

We express our anger at these abusers but we all use children for our adult needs for power, and in the guise of 'good manners' encourage the child to 'kiss uncle' regardless of his rough beard and the smell of drink on the breath.

Kissed, dangled on the knee, lifted up, pawed, and dressed up for the pleasure of the adult, not the needs of the child, who is rarely offered even the physical space to explore unhappiness without being pressed to some heaving adult bosom!

We crush the child in an embrace to deny their separateness and hurt so we the adults can feel better and deny to ourselves that children feel pain and can cope with it. We need to demystify childhood to ensure that children's rights are respected and their needs met.

Listen to the children. Different from the Victorian images. This is a playground rhyme written by girls aged 7 in London 1985.

Song

My boyfriend gave me an apple,
my boyfriend gave me a pear,
my boyfriend gave me a kiss on the lips
and threw me down the stairs.

I gave him back his apple,
I gave him back his pear,
I gave him back his kiss on the lips
and I threw him down the stairs.

He took me to the pictures,
to see a sexy film,
and when I wasn't looking
he kissed another girl.

I threw him over Italy,
I threw him over France.
I threw him over Germany
and he landed on his arse.

A New Paradigm

Prout and James (1990) suggest a new paradigm for the sociology of childhood:

(1) Childhood is understood as a social construction. As such it provides an interpretative frame for contextualising the early years of human life. Childhood, as distinct from biological immaturity, is neither a natural nor universal feature of human groups but appears as a specific structural and cultural component of many societies.

(2) Childhood is a variable of social analysis. It can never be entirely divorced from other variables such as class, gender, or ethnicity. Comparative and cross-cultural analysis reveals a variety of childhoods rather than a single and universal phenomenon.

(3) Children's social relationships and cultures are worthy of study in their own right, independent of the perspective and concerns of adults.

(4) Children are and must be seen as active in the construction and determination of their own social lives, the lives of those around them and of the societies in which they live.

Children are not just the passive subjects of social structures and processes.

(5) Ethnography is a particularly useful methodology for the study of childhood. It allows children a more direct voice and participation in the production of sociological data than is usually possible through experimental or survey styles of research.

(6) ...to proclaim a new paradigm of childhood sociology is also to engage in and respond to the process of reconstructing childhood in society.

Perhaps this paradigm could help us experience the child as first and foremost a person, not an object for concern.

Mirrors

Perpetrator and Child; Therapist and Child

Children who have been hurt and groomed for abuse by adults will find it very difficult to trust the motives of any adult. The therapist needs to consider aspects of the relationship which could confuse the child.

THE SPACE

The therapist needs to think clearly about how the child who has been groomed and seduced into a relationship with her abuser might perceive the meaning of the therapeutic space and the role of the therapist.

Abusers are magicians and seducers when they groom the child. And they use play to seduce.

The therapist offers the child a playing space out of reality time to play and make up stories to help sort out the hurt. The abuser has offered the child a special place and space out of reality time to groom the child and subsequently abuse the child.

'This is your special time' says the therapist.

'This is our special time' says the perpetrator.

I differentiate the two spaces for the child by rules and intentions. These rules are described in Chapter 2.

In the playing space, no hitting and hurting between child and therapist and no touching each other. I explain that the no touching rule is because I know the child has been hurt by a grown-up, and that I am not going to hurt her so no touching makes that clear. When the rules are defined and the child is in agreement then we begin the therapeutic process.

Abusers manipulate play; rough and tumble play to break down body boundaries or play to de-sensitise the child are grooming tactics. So for the child the similarities between the process of play and the process of grooming for abuse can create confusion. They are different processes: one to heal, the other to corrupt, but clear boundaries must be maintained.

The therapist must constantly keep self-monitoring to maintain the clarity of the therapeutic process and the creativity of the space to hold the difference. The therapist contains this space, a physical and emotional space, and does not smother the child physically or emotionally – as the abuser has done. To achieve this the therapist must constantly reflect on her own emotional processes, through training, supervision and personal therapy.

CONFIDENTIALITY/SECRETS

The child who is abused enters into a world of secrets with her abuser. The need for secrecy can also be surrounded by threats about the consequences of 'telling', so for such a child to discriminate confidentiality from secrets is complex and stressful.

It is important to help the child understand that she is in control of her own therapeutic material and can choose to tell whom she pleases, and that decisions of whom to tell belong to the child.

Threats made by the abuser about the consequences of telling can corrupt the therapeutic space. One abuser threatened to cut the throat of the child, aged 4, if she told anybody of the abuse and he said that he would cut the throat of the person she told as well. So the child carried this fear and responsibility that both she and I would be killed by this man. A boy abusing his younger brother said that nobody would believe him if he told. A baby sitter said the children would get into trouble if they told.

All this is tested in the playing space and we need to reframe these threats in a better narrative so the child does not take responsibility for the perpetrator's actions.

Keeping the Therapist Safe

The Biggest Monster in the World

The Skeleton, the Snake and the Wolf all lived together and sometimes when they were in a bad mood they fought.

The biggest monster in the world came and the skeleton, the snake and the wolf had swords.

They fought and they fought and they fought and screamed and screamed.

And the big monster tried to kill herself but couldn't do it.

Because she was so nice she realised she wasn't monster after all.

She threw off her mask and her fingernails and said:

'I'm free at last'.

The End.

Messing with monsters is a difficult and corrupting business. We need to own our own abusive natures and it is painful when the child perceives the monster in us and tests our capacity to hurt. If we deny our vulnerability then we become dangerous and cruelty can overwhelm us.

There are many dangers. The therapist, like the child, can accommodate to abuse and become inured to new horrors so that the child becomes 'just another case' and the loss of individuality which is the consequence of abuse is reinforced by the therapist.

The therapist's desire to take the hurt away can tempt her to minimise the hurt, or smother the child with nurture so that the pain is never explored and resolved because it is too hard for the adult to accept that such cruelty exists and she can't bear to hear it from the child. The desire to rescue the child can lead the therapist to action before thinking of the consequences for the child.

The therapist must remain constantly alert to the dynamics of abuse so that she doesn't feed into the system.

Chasing the Monstrous Others

From a Humument

life is

elements

that

contact,
united,

evil losing its meaning
the good losing
the evil. Hence
the fact

of the other.

Tom Phillips

There are monsters everywhere. Picasso said:

'If one were to trace a line linking all the places where I've lived in my life one might end up with the drawing of a Minotaur.' (Giraudy 1988, p.26)

So can we chase that monster in the therapeutic space? Catch as catch can in the playing and the stories and the roles we can take.

We can attack the monster in his den, dare to enter the labyrinth, that mysterious place built to house the monster; follow him so you don't lose him.

Or you can, as with everything in these encounters, use the mirror image and reverse the labyrinth so you follow the monster to *avoid* encountering him.

Like the pantomime shout of 'He's behind you' as we chase around in the light and in the dark.

This is Mandy's monster. She was 8 when she described him.

Mr Slimy

There was once a monster called Mr Slimy.

He was purple.

He ate people, and slime for breakfast, dinner, tea and he especially liked black people because they tasted nice.

He ate slugs and snails and he shouted and hit.

He made a huge roar and went munch and crunch.

Her response to this monster had been to become an elective mute: Don't talk, don't think, don't get eaten.' She chose the reverse chase: follow the monster so you avoid meeting him.

When Mandy was silent *she* became the other, the monster who wouldn't engage. Wipe out the rest of the world so you can rule it without caring for anyone else.

Ravi's experience of the monster was a feeling of fear about the house and land of the monster as well as love and fear for the monster himself.

The Story of the One Eyed Vampire

The Vampire lived in a spooky castle.

It was all horrible with ghosts and other vampires.

There lived a vampire in another castle and they are fighting over who would be the leader of the world.

Their world is slime and sand mixed.

There are bad areas and peaceful areas.

Their world is slime and sand mixed.

The sand is the peaceful place and the slime is the bad place.

In the slime, sexy things happen to children.

And hitting.

This destroys all the other good things like houses and castles.

The good place is where there is nature, houses and good food.

There is a river between the good land and the bad land and the good people try to keep the Vampires away.

The good people go to the river and take action to help the hurt children in the bad lands cross the river and get to the good land.

Ravi says that the Vampires are still all powerful and sometimes it is not clear what action the good people must take to keep them away. Anyway, who are the good people?

As we catch and catch can with monsters, some monsters do get caught.

The Monster Caught

Once upon a time there was a monster called Dexter and he lived in prison because he had been nasty to David.

Dexter was sent straight to prison and he bit a policeman.

Dexter said 'I am going to hurt you in a minute' and he said 'shit' to the policeman and he went straight away and pushed him.

Dexter fell over, banged his head and cried and he stayed in prison.

Baudrillard (1993) says,

'Each of us lives by setting traps for the other.'

And the child still asks:

'Am I the other? Am I the monster?'

We Are All Monsters

There was once a crocodile who was really angry.

He'd got it really bad.

He said 'bastard,' and 'fart' and 'stink' and 'poo'.

He said all those things because he was angry.

He wanted to bite David and Ann and David's mum and dad.

David's mum and dad said 'shit,'

David said 'shit' too.

Ann said 'shit' and they said

'I am going to hurt you' to the crocodile.

David said that he is an idiot.

David said he's full of shit especially in his tummy.

He has a ton of shit in his belly.

David wants to know how he is going to get rid of his shit.

That ton of shit in his tummy.

In the house, out of the house, round the house. The monster chases us, then we turn into monsters. So in the story, David and David's mum and dad and Ann, while being chased by the monster crocodile, say 'shit' and become the monsters. Then they start hunting the crocodile. But being a monster is a heavy burden. You end like David, carrying a 'ton of shit in his belly'. The drama goes on. Is there a way through the labyrinth? Maybe. Never a really happy ending, but possibility.

Mark wrote about his monster five years on from his abuse. He was twelve when he told this story:

'This is an evil face. It is hidden somewhere.

It doesn't belong to anyone.

It has a beard, flushed cheeks, cold lips.

It scares people away, kills people, and eats them and abuses them.

The evil one spews blue evil.

It dribbles from his mouth and from his eyes.

This poisons anyone who touches it and they die a horrible painful death.

All the children get eaten by slime or the monster or suffocated by slime.

Some children might get free but others are lost for ever. Drowned by evil.

Only two escaped.

They grew up.

They lived in a wild wood in a forest.

They made a hut, only each other for company.

They don't want a family.

Just to survive.

In the end they go back home to England.

They get a house and their friends live with them.

Much later they married and had children.

They learnt to be good parents by going to school to learn.

Because their own parents had left when they were very young and nobody else had shown them how.'

The Therapist through the Labyrinth

And what are the memories for the therapist who enters the labyrinth and meets the child?

We are haunted by the children's stories; sometimes it all seems hopeless, sometimes there is joy when the child finds joy.

The knowledge and pain of the hurt done to children seeps into the soul

Baudrillard (1993) says:

'Childhood haunts the adult universe as a subtle and deadly presence. It is in this sense that the child is other to the adult: the child is the adult's destiny, the adult is his most subtly distilled form. The child nevertheless repudiates the adult all the while moving within him with all the grace of those who have no will of their own.'

Bird woman

Once there was a child who sprouted wings. They sprang from her shoulder blades, and at first they were vestigial. But they grew rapidly, and in no time at all she had a sizeable wing span. The neighbours were horrified. 'You must have them cut' they said to her parents. 'Why?' said her parents, and this seemed so final that the neighbours left. But a few weeks later the neighbours were back. 'If you won't have them cut off at least have them clipped.' 'Why?' said the parents. 'Well at least it shows that you are doing something.' 'No' said the parents, and the neighbours left. Then for the third time the neighbours appeared. 'On at least two occasions you have sent us away,' they informed the parents 'but think of that child. What are you doing to the poor little thing?' 'We are teaching her to fly,' said the parents quietly.

Feminist Fables Namjoshi, S.

CHAPTER 4

Stories of Fear and Loathing

'To be born is to be wrecked on an island' J.M. Barrie

'She told my da and I got killed. He didn't give me a chance to deny it… He used his belt. He didn't wear a belt. He kept it just for this. The back of my legs. The outside of my hand that was trying to cover my legs. The arm that he held onto was sore for days after. Round in a circle in the living room. Trying to get well in front of the sweep of the belt so it wouldn't hurt as much. I should have done it the other way, backed into the belt, given him less room to swing. Everyone else in the house was crying, not just me. The whistle of the belt; he was trying to get in a good shot. Messing, playing with me, that was what he was doing. Then he stopped. I kept moving, jerking ahead; I didn't know he'd stopped for good. He let go of my arm, and I noticed the pain there. Up where it joined the shoulder, it was very sore there. I was heading into uncontrollable sobs. I didn't want that; I didn't enjoy it any more. I held my breath. It was over. It was over.'

Roddy Doyle (1993) *Paddy Clarke Ha Ha Ha*

Children who have been hurt by adults and come for Play Therapy, want a space to express their hurt and try to make some meaning for themselves about the pain and the fear. They need to be able to express their loathing and their love for those who hurt them.

It is a complex process for young children and they need their grief to be heard by an adult who can accept their story and explore, together with them, the paradox of loving someone who is also, at times, a monster.

If the abuse has been sexual, there may be images, arousal states, enacted scenarios, pain and terror to deconstruct, and the sense that the child too is a monster because they were part of those scenarios. There is often a strong loyalty to those who hurt. There was the fun of secrets and the power that being the holder of secrets can bring to the child. The fun of being special, the gifts, the attention. The child needs a space to express regret and loss as well as anger and hurt.

A story or a narrative is a way for the child to convey some of those conflicts and with the therapist as listener try to negotiate a shared interpretation of events. Trying to make sense of fearful events can be difficult for the child but also very difficult for many members of the child's immediate social world, because new knowledge, ideas and explanations may have to be negotiated, so that anger and disgust are not heaped back on the child.

The work of understanding and making meaning about the abuse must be shared with those who care for the child so that there is an integrated narrative of what has happened.

Play to Explore Meaning

For the child, play is a place to explore meaning. Vygotsky (1978) stated that in play, action is subordinated to meaning, but in real life, action dominates meaning. Therefore to consider play as a prototype of a child's everyday activity and its predominant form is completely incorrect.

In one sense a child at play is free to determine his own actions but in another sense this is an illusory freedom, for his actions are subordinated to the meanings of things, and he acts accordingly. The primary paradox of play is that the child operates with an alienated meaning in a real situation.

Another important factor in the process of exploring meaning through storytelling and narratives is that it can act partly as a cooling function. While telling a story can revive a strong experience, it does not usually create the same intensity of feeling as the actual experience. The creation of a story where the events and characters are similar but 'not me' also creates an effect of distance from the terror and trauma of the actual events.

In sexual abuse, the perpetrator often sets ups structures like a performance, and the child becomes actor in these sequences. In Play Therapy the child is able to reconstruct those scenarios in narrative form so they can be reframed and made less fearful.

I recall a story by an 11-year-old girl describing a frightening experience where her abuser had placed a handkerchief over her face so she couldn't see what was happening to the rest of her body. This was reframed in the story form with Arnold Schwarzenegger as the 'monster'. The event was contained in the fiction of the story and became tolerable.

In this story form, the girl suffocated and died, so the ultimate terror was expressed, the worst possible scenario constructed, and it was bearable. Arnold drowned in slime. A terror was heard and contained. And because it was play and fiction, the death of Arnold in the slime became light-hearted. And the world turned and we survived to go on playing together. So the story is the container.

Engel (1995) stated that a story must convey some sense of subjective experience, either by describing the hero's consciousness or by including a protagonist capable of intentions and feelings. Stories balance a relationship among author, text, and audience.

At the less well-formed end of the continuum there may be narratives without qualifying as full-fledged stories having only approximated towards the criteria. So

'This is Barry picking his nose.
He is saying "Yum, yum" and eating snot'
'Tum, yum,
Stick it up your bum, bum'

could well be defined as the unformed end of the storytelling spectrum! However, it is a beginning story, to test the relationship between child and therapist, checking what is acceptable, demonstrating in the tone and intonation of the speaking a self-loathing which emerged forcefully as the relationship and storymaking progressed.

This connection between storyteller and listener can be another way of exploring the different spheres of potential meanings in a child's story. First there is the child's explicit story to be considered, then the meanings it evokes in her. Then the story that the listener hears, and the meanings that story evokes for the listener.

In that way we can map out these four different worlds of meaning. This mapping is mediated between the child and therapist by describing what the story evokes for each of them and this can be a useful process for the child who is trying to construct complex life events into a helpful story.

So Barry's story evoked shock, horror, disgust, laughter, self-loathing and we sorted which emotion belonged to whom in the here-and-now of the dramatic presentation of the story. So began the exploration of identity; who am I and who are you, what feelings and thoughts do we share about the story and which are different?

Children's Stories of Fear and Loathing

These are some stories told by children who have experienced terror and pain. In play they were able to make stories and narrations about their experiences and alleviate some of their pain.

The struggle goes on for these children. Their environment can change because of life events; they lose their birth family but may become trapped in the care system. So the stress is compounded, and the loss and hurt seem never ending.

Like the old Scottish story *The Battle of The Birds*:

> So the king's son married Auburn Mary and the wedding lasted long and all were happy.

But all I got was butter on a live coal, porridge in a basket, and paper shoes for my feet, and they sent me for water to the stream, and the paper shoes came to an end.

Brian

Brian was a 5-year-old boy. He was referred to me after he had disclosed sexual abuse by his father. He had been in foster care for some months because of physical abuse by his father, and an accusation of the sexual abuse by his father had been made to the police by Brian's aunt. Brian was in foster care preparing to go and live with his mother who had been forced to leave him when he was about one year old. His father had not allowed Brian's mother to see him since that time.

I saw Brian 10 times, quite intensively while he was in foster care and then made three visits when he was living with his mother. Throughout this time I worked with his mother so she could support Brian. The interventions were focused on the sexual abuse he had experienced. All his stories contained very crude language which was how his father spoke to him as he set up abuse scenarios. Brian wanted to try to make some sense of these incidents which was difficult for such a young child.

I met Brian and suggested we might play together and make up stories because I had heard what he had said about his father. Brian said that it was scary with his dad when he did the hurting things. I explained about telling stories in play and 'I bet you the same thing has happened to people in your stories as has happened to you'. Brian said he would enjoy seeing me. He was an articulate boy, curious and interested in all the play materials.

I explained the rules of our playing together. He found rules irksome because he wanted to control all social interactions so he was always testing the boundaries, especially time boundaries. He wanted to control the endings.

He was very clear that he could play about 'rude' things on my mat and he kept that boundary well and the crude language was contained in the playing space. We shared the conversation about rules with his carers so he knew he could talk about his play to them and his mother if he chose. Our play was not a secret.

At the first meeting, Brian spent a lot of time in messy play. He loved slime and it was always his favourite activity. Then he made up a story. The hero in all his stories was called Luke.

The Fizzy, Fizzy Monster

There was once a monster called Fizzy, Fizzy monster and he breaks things up.

He eats the gunge.

He bites people.

One day he took the slime home with him and ate it all.

He lives in London.

He lives with his dad and his mum who are also monsters too.

They try and eat the gunge with him.

The monster mum and dad are kind to the monster and to Brian.

Fizzy, Fizzy monster is kind to Ann and Brian and he doesn't bite them or do nasty things to other people.

He takes people's things.

His mum is a wriggly wriggly worm and he is not really a monster but a wriggly wriggly worm.

The monster eats slime.

It's made of 'fuck' slime like kicking arse holes and kicking monster willy off.

Just make it and slosh it in his face.

Slosh fuck slime in his face and wee and poo and fuck, fuck the monster.

You just bite it up.

This is his mum eating willy.

It is green.

'Do you want to eat this' my dad is saying?

The two monsters said 'This is very rude'

They said 'fuck off'

They said 'willy, willy, fuck off, fuck off.

The ceiling is cracking 'fuck off'.

When Brian began to talk about the 'fuck' slime he began to repeat phrases in a mimicking way. Brian said that his dad had taught him to say the rude words when they were playing being rude together and with dad's girlfriend whom he called 'mum'.

We decided that the monsters in the story were very naughty to use such swear words and to be rude and sexy with children. We would be quite scared if we met them.

We did a bit of sorting about 'private parts' of the body. I gave Brian some basic biological information about sex using the illustrations from *Where Did I Come From* (Mayle 1978) to contextualise the abuse and explain why grown-ups get so intense, angry and embarrassed about such matters.

Brian started his story about monsters who were nasty but then as he explored further he was more explicit about their sexual monstrousness. He felt safe enough to try to explore this a little in the containment of the story form. We discussed why the words he used were called 'swear' words.

The story in the next session continued the theme. No gradual exploration just straight to the sexual abuse. Children often change their gender as they explore hurt; a distancing mechanism. So he becomes she.

There is a baby who is hiding in the fuck, fuck, willy slime.

The nasty monster is trying to find her.

He found her.

He put the little girl in a tub.

He didn't hit her or hurt her.

   'I'm trying to cut the willy up.

   Dad's willy for the mum to eat'.

The dad said

   'I know. fuck, fuck, willy bum, bum, poo'.

Daddy is touching his own willy and the little boy's.

Luke gets the little girl out and shouts at the monster

   'what are you doing to my little girl?'

The monster's gone away now.

Luke has put him in the bin.

Brian was abused by his father in the bathroom and by his father and girlfriend in the bedroom. We explored being scared of the monster and all the words they were saying. And the fear for the children of what might happen next. Brian asked me to take the monsters home with me and throw them in the rubbish. I said that I would. And I did.

   The story continued in the third session;

   The monster is eating gunge.

   This gunge is fuck, fuck, willy.

   This is a fuck, fuck, willy house.

   This monster looks after the fuck, fuck, willy house.

   In this house everybody is naughty.

   They say 'fuck off'.

Brian finished the story and said he wanted to tell me what his daddy had done to him.

   He described the sexual abuse he had experienced, how much it had hurt, and how scared he was by the way his daddy and daddy's girlfriend had talked.

We again talked about respect for people's bodies and that grown-ups shouldn't hurt children in this way, and about how brave it was for him to tell his aunt when he was so afraid. He was scared of all the rude words and the laughing and the hurting. We found a poem about scary dads. We liked the rhyme and the picture by Colin McNaughton

When A Dinosaur Dad Comes Home From Work

Be nice to Dad when he comes home
(Of course he'd never beat you!).
But if he's had a tiring day
He might just up and eat you!

Brian wanted to do a drawing in my story book to show how naughty his daddy was. We agreed and I wrote that daddy was naughty because grown-ups shouldn't abuse children's bodies.

Brian wanted the story safe in my book. He said that if he lived in that naughty house, would he be naughty too? We worked out that you don't have to be naughty just because grown-ups have hurt you.

The next story was called Willy Wonkers.

Willy Wonkers

Once upon a time there were a lot of willies and they lived in a willy.

This willy belongs to a good man who doesn't show it to little boys and hurt them.

We put all the naughty willy and put them in a box so they would keep safe.

My dad's willy was there and it was green.

There are loads and loads of willys.

Some are good but they have been naughty.

They have hurt people.'

The theme of containment of the abuse developed as the sessions continued – keeping physical boundaries, no hitting or hurting and respect for each other's bodies.

There had been a lot of physical restraint when Brian was abused. His hands were tied up and he was frightened of the physical proximity of adults.

Brian continued to try to control the adults in his social world to prevent hurt or alternatively to get adults angry quickly to get the hurt over and done with.

He became less demanding as he began to trust those who were caring for him.

Brian moved to live with his mother and her partner. A new situation, a new world to understand. He tried to control their world. He wouldn't got to bed, he wouldn't accept the rules of the household but they coped with this and he settled with them. He had moved a considerable distance from his familiar surroundings to live with his mother and he felt the loss of his dad's family.

Feeling safe with his mother would take a long time. His mother had left when he was little, the next 'mother' sexually abused him with dad. His dad farmed him out to members of the family so he had never experienced a settled family life.

At his mother's house, Brian told his last story about the slime.

The Slime Fuck

There was a pile of fuck slime and it was scary, horrible and fuck.

Slime fuck was on the mat and a big van went through it.

Then a man walked through it.

There is good slime too and it is OK to sit in there.

Luke walked through the bad slime and it is pulling him back which is why it's back a bit.

Luke is very sensible because he walks through the slime with his wellies on and doesn't get hurt.

Luke is safe now because he's in the good slime.

The green slime is OK but it's like a puddle.

In fact it is a puddle.

Brian was proud of his strategies in this story, especially the trick of keeping his wellies on so walking through slime wouldn't contaminate. His biggest worry was always that he was naughty because he had lived in the 'fuck, fuck, willy house'.

We thought that to live in the scary house had been a problem but now he didn't live there any more and anyway he hadn't been naughty when he had lived there. Brian was beginning to express ideas about good events as well as scary events.

Life began to change. Brian went to Nursery School. He made new friends. He had the dog to think about and look after and a garden to play in.

I came to visit for the last time. Brian made up a story about a dinosaur; no slime this time, but a very short story. It was painful for both of us to say good-bye; we had shared some frightening memories but we needed to leave the cage and fly free.

'Once upon a time there was a dinosaur who ran away.

But then he came back and was put in a cage.

He didn't mind being shut in a cage.

Then a big green dragon flew down and got the dinosaur out of the cage.

The End.'

It is difficult for the therapist to work with such stories, not only for the explicit sexual content but because of the language which the child has been taught. It provokes anxiety. Should the therapist stay with this exploration?

Although Brian was very young he was clear that the play space was where he could make these stories with the echoes of the scary scenes of sexual abuse.

He wanted the containment, but he wanted to be heard. He wanted somebody to take away the rubbish of his past and he wanted to know that not everybody who lived in the monstrous house was a monster.

As Brian gets older he may need to rework his ideas about the abuse he experienced. He understood what he could for a child of five years of age. Who knows yet if mother and son can make a reasonable attachment. Does Brian feel valued enough to throw off the contamination of abuse?

So far, so good, but still only so far.

Mandy

Mandy had been physically abuse by the adults in her family and sexually abused by her elder brothers. When I met her she was eight years old.

Mandy had found a way to control her social world. She became a elective mute, speaking when it pleased her and being silent if she wanted to control the interaction.

Mandy was to be adopted in a family. She liked it there and felt safe. She had lived with them for a year. She was doing well at school but her birth parents are English and African and the adoptive family are white. The purpose of the intervention was to give Mandy a space to reflect on her present circumstances. It was to be a brief intervention. Eight sessions.

Mandy liked play. Some times when we met she would speak, other times she would play with her back to me. One time she played away for the play area so I ignored her and began to do some work as I sat on the mat. Mandy became furious and returned to play immediately, demanding my full attention. I said it was catch as catch can. See what it feels like from the other end of the telescope.

As Mandy played and made stories I sometimes asked her questions as she made her narratives. My questions are written in italics in her stories.

In the first session, Mandy began to play with slime and a monster figure. She put slime in the mouth of the monster.

'There was once a monster called Yellow Head and one day all his skin fell off through his eyes, mouth and brain.

His skin was pink which was funny because he was yellow.

He felt scared when his skin fell off.'

The theme of Mandy's identity as a black person emerged in story form throughout the sessions. To think pink but be yellow. Which world to inhabit? The fear of exposure was a constant theme. Exposure for Mandy was fearful because her form of coping was to conceal not peel away.

She began to narrate unsafe/safe places. She put some figures in a sand tray and made up this story.

'This is car land.

What kind of place is it?

It is a very nasty place because it is scary.

There are eight cars and a monster who tries to get the cars to eat them up.

There are people in the cars who are very scared of getting eaten by the monster.

Who is the monster?

The crocodile monster is the snake's friend.

The snake kills the people in the cars and then the crocodile monster eats them

Crocodile monster eats people and cars and sand.

What happens to the people?

All the people get dead.

What happens to the monsters?

The snake and the crocodile monster just go on making the place bad.

Why are the snake and the crocodile monsters?

The snake and the crocodile are brothers.

The snake is the elder one.

What happens when they have eaten everyone?

When they have everything they just wait until other people come along and then they will eat them.

This is not a nice place to live.'

We decided that there was no appeasing these monsters. Their world was just not a place to inhabit.

Mandy made another world in the sand.

'This is a safe place.

Water, sand, mermaids.

The mermaids lie buried in case the crocodile finds them again.

The End.'

So even in the safe place you have to have strategies to keep safe and the strategy is to stay hidden.

This was another theme. Hiding, disguising, not showing or revealing. Mandy made up many stories about mermaids and monsters: those who hid and those who hurt.

She usually created a world in a sand tray to structure her stories.

The Mermaids

Ariel.

This mermaid is brown, she is a daughter and her life has been good and bad.

Where does she live?

She lives in the sea.

What's it like?

It's cold sea.

Does she like it there?

She really likes it there.

What has been bad in her life?

She never talks about the bad things because it is too scary.

Why?

She thinks if she talks or even thinks about the bad things she will fall to pieces in the sea.

And then what?

And the shark will eat her up.

Mandy's mermaids always had ways to protect themselves. Hiding, swimming, burying themselves in sand; strange brown creatures, not quite human, not quite fish, swimming in a cold sea.

Then there were the monsters. The Yellow monsters were a threat to the mermaids.

The Yellow Monsters

The yellow monster lives in the sea and he looks horrible.

How is he monstrous?

This monster is not doing sexy stuff but hitting stuff.

Who does he hit?

He hits all the mermaids.

And they are scared he'll come and get them.

Why?

He said he would get them, beat them up and beat up the people they told.

Then a return to the snake and the crocodile and the theme of brother monsters.

Snake and Crocodile

The naughty monster and the naughty snake are doing hitting things.

The are bad brothers.

Then the Purple Slime Monster who, however fearful, is missed. And a sense of mistrust towards those who might help.

The Purple Slime Monster

The purple slime monsters howled in the slime.

Then one day he got out and he ate every single person that he saw.

The slime made farty noises because it missed the monster.

The monster howls in the purple slime.

Why?

He is warning everyone.

What about?

He is a hitting monster.

Who does he hit?

He likes little girls and wants to hurt them.

What do the little girls do?

'They must hide, run away or tell the police or the people who look after them if you can trust them'.

Then Dragon Country solely inhabited by monsters. At least the mermaids don't live in this world.

Dragon Country

This is dragon country ruled by the dragon.

The snake lives there as well.

They are both bosses of this country.

They are not related.

They are just friends.

The girl doesn't live there.

The baby doesn't live there.

And the mermaid doesn't live there.

Just the dragon and the snake.

Nobody wants to go there because of the snake and the dragon

They do horrible things.

Then the most fearful monster held in a pile of snot.

The noisiest snot in the world held a man.

He is naughty, sexy naughty and hitting naughty.

What's his name?

He is too scary to have a name.

Is he old or young?

He is grown up and called we don't know what.

Why is he in the slime?

Mandy put him in the slime because he is so bad.

What will happen to him?

You can't get rid of monsters but you can bury them.

Will he get out?

If he ever got out, Mandy would put him back in again.

Would she be angry with him?

She would never speak to him about what he had done.

Why not?

He has magicked her into silence.

What happens if she speaks?

If she speaks something terrible will happen.

If she speaks she will get killed.

   How?

She will be chopped into pieces by a knife.

That is why she is so silent.

   Can anybody help her?

Nobody can stop it happening.

Then back to the two monsters and the fear of telling.

The Bad Men

There are two bad men riding fierce, strange tiger animals.

They are all bad.

They are going out to kill people.

Everybody is afraid of them.

They are very angry people.

They are the people who cut up children if they tell.

This time they go out but they don't find anybody to hurt.

Mandy created these stories by placing toys and objects in a sand tray, describing the images, waiting for me to ask questions about the characters. The stories came flooding out one after the other in a series of sessions.

After the monster stories we had two no talking meetings. Mandy sat with her back to me or turned round and sat handling the toys and materials in a desultory fashion. Sitting, turning away, turning back, touching the toys, putting them away, turning away, watching me to see my reaction to her silence. I waited, Mandy waited, we both watched, Mandy turned her back…and the dance began again.

It is not easy to stay comfortable with silence, to wait, to dance, to stay yourself, not to make demands.

The next session brought a change of theme, that of Mandy ruling the world. She drew a picture of a rainbow with Mandy standing on the top and all her friends below looking up at her on the rainbow. This is a narration we made together about the picture.

Once there was once a rainbow,

and some children stood underneath it.

Who is standing on top of the rainbow?

On top of the rainbow stood Mandy.

What was the rainbow like?

The rainbow was just pretty.

It didn't keep you safe, or help, but it was pretty.

What did Mandy feel like?

On top of the rainbow,

Mandy felt King of the World.

Which is what she wanted to be.

What did the children feel like?

The children below were scared of her because she was so bossy.

Does Mandy mind being so alone?

No, no, no.

Mandy wanted badly to be king.

She doesn't care.

So there!

Mandy had a strong definition of self and what she wanted. She was clear that now was not the time she felt safe enough to explore her hurtful past. The abuse and threats were still too frightening to be explored and she was not sure how 'safe' she needed to be; but not yet. She felt part of her adoptive family and was attached but she still felt separate and different. She felt that being a black girl in her social world exposed her to hurt and isolation.

When speech was bearable, we spoke about these things. But she was doing well at school and enjoyed the love she received from her adoptive family. They were conscious of being a white family caring for a black girl and the issues were not pushed aside. Mandy had taken the time to play very seriously but now wanted to concentrate on family and school.

She was communicating well at home and school with occasional 'off' days. Her last stories were a declaration of self and an evaluation of her present situation. Being somebody takes a lot of time and effort.

No Name

There was once a black girl called No Name,

 and she was nice.

What did she look like?

She had beautiful black hair tied with colourful ribbon.

She likes her hair like that.

What did she feel like?

It makes her feel a feeling but she didn't want to tell.

She wore snot shoes and socks but the shoes smelt sweaty

And this made her feel different from all the other children.

So what happened?

Because she was different she decided to be better than everybody else.

She was good at absolutely everything.

Maths, music, reading, running, singing, acting.

She was not good at English, History, Physical Education, Religious Education and French.

She came top of the class in all the things she was good at.

So No Name was angry because she was different

And that's why she worked hard.

Because she is angry.

The End.

P.S. She can't have a name yet so she will stay angry which is in some ways good because it is a reason for her to work hard.

But one day she will have a name but not just yet.

No Voice

No Name's best friend is a girl called No Voice who doesn't speak.

Why not?

Because if she spoke her story would be so terribly sad that she would be afraid.

So No Voice has no voice.

She's good at school too.

Really The End.

No Name and No Voice felt they would achieve both Name and Voice in a loving family and with success at school. Mandy's evaluation of No Name and No Voice's academic progress mirrored her own. She knows she has fears about her past but now is not the time for that; she wants a settled family life. Enough is enough for the moment.

We enjoyed this final poem together.

A Female Rip-Tail Roarer

You just ought to see me rigged out in my best.

My bonnet is a hornet's nest,

garnished with wolves' tails and eagles' feathers.

My gown's made of a whole bear's hide, with the tail for a train.

I can drink from the branch without a cup,

shoot a wild goose flying,

wade the Mississippi without getting wet,

out scream a catamount,

and jump over my own shadow.

Anon

Katherine

I had seen Katherine and her sister before they were adopted to help them sort out the physical abuse they had experienced from their parents, especially their mother. Katherine was five at that time.

Katherine had been very afraid and was glad to be in the safety of her adoptive home. Her response to abuse was to become frozen and accepting of whatever happened to her and she felt that if she got angry she might blow up the whole world.

Katherine and the family said that they would like to be able to see me if the need arose in the future. This was agreed. Two years later Katherine said she would like to see me as she was feeling a little anxious. We met and shared news of the past two years in her family. Katherine said that she felt settled but sometimes she felt strange, not quite part of the family. She made up this story:

The Race of the Power Rangers

Ann says 'Come on Pink, Power Rangers.

Let's go now Pink Power Ranger.

Let's go for it'.

She runs so fast that she leaves everybody else.

Everybody else knows that Pink Power Ranger was a person really but had this stuff to protect her when she was really frightened.

I don't believe everybody else who knows she is a person but Ann.

Ann knows.

One day Ann sees Pink Power Ranger and realises she is a person.

> 'Just press my button on my belt and then whoosh, I become a person and it's the same for the others'

> *What is a person?*

A person is somebody who is kind and has magic.

I suppose you have to have a mum and dad to be a person.'

The End.

We talked about the rules of the adoptive family and how difficult it is sometimes to understand how to behave when you just can't trust these new parents not to hurt you.

On the second visit Katherine narrated this story:

The Golden River

This is a golden river and a river of magic pink stones

And a river of magic blue stones.

And light pink stones.

Someone called Katherine is standing in the golden river and she fell over in it and got her dress wet.

The stones dried up the dress and then Katherine was pushed over again.

They wondered why Katherine wasn't dead.

But it was the magic stones.

Katherine used objects in the toy bag to create these magic stones. You needed to have magic to become a person and the stones were the things that saved you from being swept over and drowned in this Golden River. This is the problem.

Golden rivers are all very well but sometimes a small girl can be washed away and pushed aside in the flood of gold which is too much and can overwhelm. When you are used to very little, a flood of gold can be too much.

After these visits Katherine was satisfied. She had wanted to tell me that this journey to be a 'somebody' was not easy and a kind family can be as exhausting as a scary family and sometimes it was difficult to separate the two. She said that she had a bit of magic like the girl in the Golden River and she felt safe enough in the family. I gave her a stone to keep.

A year later Katherine asked to see me again. She had been disturbed by some bad dreams and there had been a bit of a falling out with friends. She was enjoying doing work at school and it was OK with mum and dad although she felt fearful when she was told off.

When dad shouted she remembered her birth mum who screamed and shouted and threw her against a wall so hard that her shoulder got broken.

She was dreaming of dragons.

> 'They eat me up, shout, blow fire.
> Like mum telling me off'.

We made up a story about a dragon family.

The Dragon Family

There was once a dragon family.

The mum and dad were called Jane and John

The children were Charlotte and Elizabeth Daniel and Robert.

The mother wasn't fierce.

She looked after the children more better than the father.

He kept on shouting even when they hadn't done anything. Sometimes he did rude things.

He showed his willy.

He went to other people's houses and did rude dragon things like puff smoke onto other dragons.

The mother dragon pushed the children into walls.

The children got angry and sad.

The children ran away from this family to another land.

They found another mum and dad who were better.

and they almost lived happily ever after.

When the children were angry, they stayed inside and never talked to anyone.

When they were sad they cried.

When they were nasty to the parents they always said they were really sorry.

The End.

We explored these two families and the dread that what happened in the first family might happen in the second and decided that it was most unlikely, but you don't have to trust if you don't feel you can.

Katherine was satisfied and life goes on. It is often helpful to help untangle anxieties as they happen in the life of a child. Change is disturbing, however 'golden' that river seems to be.

Mark

I have known Mark for seven years. He is living in a foster family where he has been for several years. He is now just fifteen. I saw him when he was eight when he first came into care and again at twelve to explore issues about sexual abuse by his uncle when he lived at home. He left home when he was seven.

He likes his foster family very much and he sees his mother and other siblings on a regular basis. He wants/doesn't want to go home to his mother when he is sixteen.

Mark goes to special school. The terror of his past experiences made it difficult for him to concentrate and learn. He is teased about his school and finds this difficult.

He asked to see me when he was fourteen and he defined his situation as:

> Feeling sad generally.
>
> He feels helpless.
>
> He feels that he is spastic – thick.
>
> His brother who lives at home bullies him when he visits and his mother can't prevent it.
>
> He is worried about social relationships.
>
> He is not having bad dreams but his sadness is about the sexual abuse.

Mark enjoys drawing and storytelling and we decided to use those methods to communicate. Mark was worried about how to behave with a girl who he likes very much so we had some information sharing abut sexual matters and relationships.

It is images of sexual abuse which get in the way when he thinks about making a relationship with a girl.

We decide that friendship is the most important part of relationships; sex can wait. Mark wanted to tell a story. He drew a picture as he spoke.

The Old Village

> Once upon a time there was an old village near the woods and it was near Christmas
>
> And there was a snow storm.

In the morning the house was still there.

And it was snowing.

Two old people lived in the house.

They like it there.

And sometimes their children visited them.

One day they won the lottery and bought a house just like it.

New furniture.

A new car.

They gave the old house to the children which were grown up.

The parents gave money to do it up.

The children knocked out all the widows and put in double glazing.

They took the old door off and put in a new one.

We decided that the trick is how to make changes so old patterns don't repeat. Does putting new windows in old houses really change things?

Mark continued with another story.

A family go to climb the mountains.

They were climbing for years and years.

One day they discovered there was an old man sitting on the top of the mountain.

They found the cave and chatted to that old man.

He said he'd been up there for years and years and years and years.

They took the old man home and looked after him.

The End.

Is that it?

They never went climbing again.

The old man went on holiday to Australia.

He never came back.

Nobody knew what happened in Australia.

It's a mystery.

We explored lost and found and the mystery of what happens to people. What is better: being looked after in a family, sitting on top of the mountain or just to disappear and become a mystery?

The abusing uncle had disappeared after going to prison. What had happened to him? Who will care for Mark? Is home the place to be or will the past be repeated? If you don't go home will you get lost in the vastness of the world?

The next story explored sexual metaphors recalling childhood memories.

Once there was a genie who could change into anybody.

And he had a friend called Banana Man.

And Banana Man could change into a banana.

And one day genie saw a lamp and he rubbed it.

And another man came out and this time he was pink.

Genie thought it was Banana Man but it wasn't it was Pink Panther.

But Pink Panther could stretch all parts of his body.

The person was just about to eat a hot dog when he just realised it was part of Pink Panther.

It was in fact his penis.

Because when Pink Panther stretched his penis it became the longest in the world.

When it became the longest, sadly, it was so thin it looked like a fishing line.

And the genie was not impressed.

Women were also not impressed and were shocked when they saw it.

When Banana Man came back he saw Pink Panther stretched out in all parts and Banana Man said:

'You dirty man, put it away'.

Because that was his brother.

'What about you' said Pink Panther.

Banana Man said. 'I don't do the things you do.

I'm a smart guy so please leave'.

So Pink Panther went back into the genie's lamp.

And there was no more Pink Panther.'

Was sex always 'dirty', always to be associated with childhood hurt? Were these strange dream creatures always to remind him of his uncle? Would he and his brother always fight? Would they end up like uncle or violent like dad? But he had escaped by being 'thick'. His next story explored that theme.

The Nerd's Story

There was once a nerd that went to the shop and in that shop people didn't like nerds.

They were all drunken in the shop.

He wanted some crisps

and one man said

'If you do it's £3 extra.'

The nerd got angry.

'Who do you think you are talking to?

I earn more money than you.

You are just a drunk!'

Then the drunk got really angry

And he got his hand and took out both of the Nerd's eyes and made him swallow them.

The Nerd nearly died; he was just lucky enough to live.

The Nerd grew two more eyes with special vision which could see for four miles.

The eyes took a long time to function.

At first he was blind.

But with a lot of help his eyes got better.

Mark talked about the violence from his brother when he went home at the weekend. His foster carer reassured him that he didn't have to go home. We spoke with his social worker. Home got better.

The fear of being consumed continued – being consumed by abuse in the past or by a girl in the present. Like the Dark Cave.

The Dark Cave

One day there was a man walking on a path.

He went in the woods for a walk and saw this cave.

He decided to go in there.

He started to walk in but just then he looked up and found he was trapped inside.

He was fighting to get out of here but the gooey slime was trying to keep him in and kept wrapping around him.

The slime spat him out.

He quickly ran off

What did he do?

He stayed in his home and never went out because he was too frightened.

What was it like there?

He had an indoor swimming pool, golf hall, tennis hall.

It was a big mansion so he kept himself busy all day.

But the only thing was he never went out.

because he was too frightened.

We talked about the fear of dark places. I recited the children's rhyme and Mark often recites it when we meet. He recites it at night and it seems to control the bad dreams.

> In the dark, dark wood,
> There is a dark, dark, house,
> In the dark, dark house,
> There is a dark, dark, room,
> In the dark, dark, room,
> There is a dark, dark cupboard,
> In the dark, dark cupboard,
> There is a dark dark box,
> And in the dark, dark box,
> There is a *ghost*.

Mark responded with his own silly story.

A Silly Story

Jake the snake was showing off and he wanted to see how far he could go.

But he didn't know the earth was broken.

so he decided to go fast in his jeep.

He went so fast

He fell over the earth and died.

Serves him right.

Going slowly is important. You don't jump from the dark, dark wood to the dark, dark box. Go slowly and you can cope.

We have begun to explore hero characters, finding ways to be brave.

The River Thames

There is a patrol boat, life guards.

On the banks of the river are a lot of cars parked.

There was a traffic jam.

There was a police car at the very back so he overtook the other cars

He saw the cause of the jam.

It was a great big ugly monster

That had a big mouth

And a big appetite.

So he turned around and went back so fast.

The other cars couldn't believe it.

So they turned around and there was a crash.

There was a boy on a boat on the River Thames.

He was working for the life guards.

He saw the monster.

So he got off the boat and went near the monster.

And said to him;

    'Oi! you great fat slobbering, greedy, big mouthed creep

    Can't you see you are blocking up the road

    So get off.'

And he kicked him in the foot.

And the monster went crying all the way home.

    'Boo-boo.'

And everyone lived happily ever after.

And there is even hope for change from the monsters, at least in a story!

We need to contain that lost uncle who went to prison and now is – where?

The Bad-Tempered Dinosaur

There was once a very bad tempered dinosaur locked up in a cage.

And the guard said;

'Shut up, can't you see no one liked you'.

Dinosaur didn't like that at all.

So he used all his strength and managed to get out of the cage.

Everyone started running and the dinosaur even picked up a big car and threw it and it hit the guard and squashed him.

The police car came and put on the siren.

Dinosaurs don't like that noise and he ran away screaming and quickly went back to his cage.

And he was good for ever and ever.

So everyone began to like him and he had some friends.

He got fed every day.

And he even got a bigger cage.

Mark has decided to stay with his foster carers and not go and live back with his mother. She accepts his decision and he feels good about himself. He still sees his mother some weekends and holidays and the bullying from his brother has stopped. His brother has a job, which has helped.

Mark has just returned from a wonderful holiday in France with his foster family. He made friends. He still has his friend who is a girl and one day slowly, slowly, might be his girl friend. Sometimes he feels sad but not at the moment.

But the dinosaur is still caged. What is freedom? The pull of family is still strong. Which cage to choose? Does freedom mean abandonment?

Living with Parents Who Have Periods of Mental Illness

Some children who live with a parent who has periods of mental illness can experience considerable distress when the parent is ill. They may witness a psychotic episode and be confused about what has happened and what their parent was communicating to them.

Sometimes professionals working with the adults disregard the needs of the children in their sympathy for the adult. The children often take on a parenting role themselves or become the husband/wife figure for their parent. Often the needs of the children are forgotten and nobody helps the child to cope or make sense of their parent's behaviour.

Mary

Mary's mother often feels suicidal and has made attempts on her life. It is a struggle for her to look after the children. Mary, aged 8, did enjoy the opportunity to tell this story to me. She was playing with a small toy called Stretch Armstrong and was stretching his arms and legs as she spoke.

> There was once a woman called Stretch.
>
> And when she was good she was really fun.
>
> But sometimes she got really sad.
>
> And said she wanted to die.
>
> Which wasn't very nice for her friend who lived in the same house.
>
> So her friend one day stretched her and stretched her and stretched her until she was dead.
>
> Her friend Kelly said;

'There you are.

You wanted to be dead, so now you are'.

Mary quickly added:

This is a silly story.

The End.

Mary loves her mother but she needed a space to describe how horrible it can be at home. Her siblings keep her going through these horrible times and we looked at people she could tell if she felt her mum needed help.

Joshua

Joshua's mother was well and she brought Josh because he had coped with his mother's admissions to hospital in the past. She wanted him to be able to make sense of her illness. She had talked with him about the situation and supported the therapy.

It was a brief intervention and he liked the luxury of play in school time.

He made endless planets in coloured slime and inhabited them with creatures and people. His stories were about explosions of the planets. Things fall apart. How to get them back together again. The stories were repeated each week with variations. This was his favourite story:

The Big Bang

There was just a big planet with different creatures on it.

Water planet has a horse, two crocodiles and a dolphin and a turtle.

The earth planet had a hippo and one human.

The alien planet had lots of fighters.

There is a big bomb which just happens

And everything splits apart.

And they all travel to different Universes

And the planets are stretched more.

The new planets got on with earth so it didn't matter much.

There are only three universes; water, earth and the alien planet.

And they are separate but may come together again after one billion years.

But before that they learn peace

And when they meet again,

Everything moves from planet to planet

With no fighting.

The desire for peace and wholeness were dominant themes. Both mother and son share this need. To integrate the planets is so difficult to achieve when sometimes it seems out of your personal control.

Lewis

Lewis was five when I met him. His mother suffered from bouts of depression. His care was shared between his mother and a foster carer. I was asked to help him explore some frightening memories he had of his mother becoming ill.

However, immediately the work began, it was clear that his mother was not making a good recovery. The focus changed towards an assessment of the family with the social worker and psychiatrist, and the sessions were time limited. Communication between professionals was crucial for the protection of Lewis and the care of his mother. It was clear that life was difficult for Lewis and more support was put into his family. All his stories expressed anxiety about safety.

The Adventures of Good Man

One day good Man and his friend Shane were walking along when they met a skeleton.

The skeleton got tripped over and then ran away.

Then they met a witch.

They fought and fought until the witch ran away.

They were walking along and they met Shredder.

'Look' said the good man.

'The army is coming to get you.'

Shredder ran away scared.

And Good Man was pleased that he had tricked her.

A new witch came along and they began to fight again.

The witch flew away and Good Man and his friend went to bed.

When the witch was fighting she was crazy and said mad things.

She thought all her men were going to get her and fight and kill her.

Good Man was a bit scared of her because she said such crazy things.

And he thought he might die too but he didn't and neither did the witch.

When the situation at home deteriorated Lewis told this story:

The House of Horror

This is a magic house.

Sometimes when they want people to be not naughty any more it makes people not naughty by doing a spell.

What is the spell?

This is the spell.

'Issy wissy let's get busy

Let's all change to good behaviour'.

And then by magic everybody is good.

Who is the boss of the house?

The boss of the house is the dad and the mum.

There are fourteen children.

Funny, Joan, Laura, Bone Head, Stinky Sick Pant, Stinking Ravioli, Spider Man, Superman, Chinese Man, Helicopter Man, The Crazy Mask, Moaning Man, Cry Baby Man, Choo Choo Train.

The parents are called Bomber Head Dad and the mum was called Lock Head.

There was a lock on her head and you unlocked it you saw her brain and it was scary.

You would see her going crazy.

She would be mad and bounce around and be out of control.

The children locked up the mother by locking her head again.

This was a scary house to live in.

The children didn't feel safe.

Can anyone make it better?

Nobody could make it better.

It would always be scary but they could have a holiday.

They stay on holiday for twenty years and when they get back home mum and dad are still there but are very old.

The doctor looks at the lock in her head and she is better.

And anyway the children are grown up so it doesn't matter so much.

This was the time of greatest anxiety for Lewis. How nice to have fourteen siblings to help with a mother instead of coping alone.

Lewis spent more time with his foster carer and his mother was offered more help. This is his last story with me.

The Snowstorm

There was once an extra special teddy bear with a green mouth and red eyes and he was called Mr Michael Ted.

He was standing underneath a snowstorm and it was very scary.

There were green snowflakes, red snowflakes, grey snowflakes and he had nowhere to hide.

It was very dark for Mr Ted and he needed some light.

Then he saw a beautiful red candle which gave him light.

But when he looked in the light he saw an ugly monster who wanted to get the ancient mask and kill everybody in the world and beyond – that is the Universe.

Ted was scared of the monster and the snow but because he was an investigator he couldn't show he was scared.

So Ted called the Funny Man who could kill the monster and that's what the Funny Man did.

The Funny Man is a bit horrible and he let Mr Ted go free then he flooded the place with snot from his ears.

Mr Ted had to decide whether to stay in the scary place or go to the safe place but he couldn't stay in the snowy place

Because it was flooded with snot so he went to the house and field that was safe

The monster who got killed got sent up into space and the Funny Man who was a bit horrible still had loads of snot and was still alive in the next door from home to Ted's.

Mr Funny learnt to control his snot so it wouldn't get over the field and the home of the Teds.

But there will be another monster.

Read on for next time.

Lewis was living through such difficult times that changes had to be made to his environment so he felt safer and better held.

It is not really possible to reflect on the snowstorm if you are still in the middle of it and afraid that Funny Man's snot will get at you. It was not the time for therapy. There was nobody to hold Lewis's anxiety. He needed protection before therapy.

So remember, safety first and think of this poem before you rush to rescue.

Don't Call Alligator Long-Mouth Till You Cross River

Call alligator long-mouth
call alligator saw-mouth
call alligator pushy-mouth
call alligator scissors-mouth
call alligator raggedy mouth
call alligator bumpy-bum
call alligator all dem rude word
but better wait
                    till you cross river.

John Agard

CHAPTER 5

Stories of Loss and Abandonment

'She cried out for Mama, who did not
hear. She left with a wild eye thrown back.
she left with curses, rage
that withered her features to a hag's…'

Rita Dove (1995) From Persephone
Abducted in *Mother Love*

I never got the chance to run away. I was too late. He left first.
The way he shut the door; he didn't slam it. Something; I just
knew: he wasn't coming back. He just closed it, like he was
going down to the shops, except it was the front door and we
only used the front door when people came. He didn't slam
it. He closed it behind him. – I saw him in the glass. He waited
for a few seconds, then went. He didn't have a suitcase or even
a jacket, but I knew.'

Roddy Doyle (1993) From *Paddy Clarke Ha Ha Ha*

The loss of a member of the birth family is difficult for a child to
accept and to be separated from the whole family an abandonment
hard to bear. However difficult the family, however terrible the abuse
and hurt, whatever the reason for separation, to leave the past behind
and adapt to new circumstances is a gargantuan task.

How does the child attach to a new family if their early experiences of parenting have been distorted by hurt, abuse or violence? If the early experience of care is that adults terrorise or tease, torment and reject, then some of the coping strategies learnt in times of stress could be carried to the new situation where they may be redundant. This expectation of abuse and blame can create conflict and disturbance in the new family, sometimes to the point of breakdown and rejection, so there is more loss, more separation for the child to confirm their sense of worthlessness.

Attachment Theory

Bowlby's Formulation

Bowlby (1969, 1973) defined attachment as 'the bond that ties' the child to his/her primary carer and attachment behaviours are those which maintain the child in close physical proximity to the carer. If closeness is maintained then the result should be comfort and security. In a healthy attachment, there is separation upset; that is, the severance of the tie produces distress. For bonding to occur, attachment needs to be reciprocated on the part of the carer so that the attachment is mutual. Attachment behaviours such as crying, sucking, clinging, smiling, vocalising are part of a behavioural system that has a set goal of proximity to the carer. The system is activated by information concerning the child's distance from the carer.

The original function of attachment behaviours was as a protection against predators. Bowlby stated that this system is one of many behavioural systems the child possesses; other important ones are exploration, affiliation and wariness, and there is a continuous interplay of these systems with the attachment system. The child has a preference for one carer but attachment behaviour may be present with a number of carers, but there is a hierarchy of preferences.

Bowlby suggested that in the first year or two the child's attachment is very much that of seeking the physical presence of the caregiver, but in time the child comes to form an internal working model of their attachment figures. He or she develops an inner sense of the nature of those individuals as well as of the actual relationship that the child has formed with them. As the child grows older these internal models become elaborated and the child forms an internal representation of carers.

The development of an internal working model focuses on the amount of stress on the attachment system and the availability of the attachment figure to help alleviate the stress. Too much stress and lack of availability of the attachment figure can lead to an internal representation of the environment as dangerous and to the feeling that the child and others are helpless to moderate these dangers.

The consequences for the child of having such a representation of their world can be fear of exploration, uncertainty of the availability of safety, doubt about their capability to master their environment and a distrust of significant others.

Ainsworth's Formulation

Following Bowlby, Ainsworth (1978) defined attachment as

> 'a tie, bond or enduring relationship between a young child and his or her primary caretaker'

However, she emphasised the child's assessment of the relative presence of threat and security as a significant part in the balance of exploration, affiliation, wariness and attachment. A child who has confidence in the attachment relationship will feel free to explore the environment. This widens the concept of attachment to include the child's subjective sense of security and the attachment behaviours to include a sense of safety so that the child is free to explore and to make relationships with others.

In this model of attachment, the context in which the relationship happens may affect the sense of security of the child. These contextual variants include setting, preceding events, the child's mood, the child's developmental level. Ainsworth (1978) developed a standardised laboratory procedure known as the Strange Situation to assess individual differences in attachment. This consisted of a series of brief standardised episodes that take place in a laboratory observation room unfamiliar to the infant. The episodes include being with the mother, being confronted by a strange adult, being left with the stranger by the mother, being left entirely alone and being reunited with the mother.

Children's reactions to the situation can be classified into three types of attachment behaviour in the Strange Situation. These are:

CATEGORY B

Secure attachment, child shows moderate level of proximity-seeking behaviour to mother.

Upset by her departure, greets her positively on return.

CATEGORY A

Insecurely attached avoidant when the child avoids contact with the mother, especially on her return after separation.

Not greatly upset when left with a stranger.

Ignores parent on reunion, focuses on toys or environment throughout procedure.

CATEGORY C

Insecurely attached resistant when the child is greatly upset when separated from the mother.

Preoccupied with parent throughout procedure.

On her return difficult to console, both seeks comfort and resists it.

A fourth group – disorganised/disoriented – was added by Main and Weston (1981; Main and Solomon 1990).

CATEGORY D

When the child displays disorganised/disoriented behaviours in the mother's presence suggesting lapse of behavioural strategy. For example, the child may freeze with a trance-like expression, hands in the air, or may move away from the parent to the wall, turning the head away while crying.

Disorganised/disorientated behaviour, in contrast to the other classifications, seems to reflect a collapse in strategy. Main (1994) suggests that this outcome should be expected if the attached child has been frightened by the parent, rather than simply by the external situation.

> 'Because the infant inevitable seeks the parent when alarmed, parental behaviour which frightens an attached infant places the infant in an irresolvable paradox in which it can neither approach (the B and C strategies) shift its attention (the A strategy) or flee (Main & Hesse, 1990/92). In keeping with this hypothesis, the great majority of parentally maltreated children (@80%) have been found to fit to the D category (see Main & Soloman 1990, for review).' (p.6)

The Child's Understanding of Meaning and Emotion in Relationships

Attachment theory emphasises the carer/child relationship in terms of functional adaptation to the environment without much emphasis on the construction of meaning between the child and carer.

The emphasis on secure/insecure aspects of a relationship, almost always the mother, excludes other aspects of the relationship between mother and child and the influence of other relationships within and beyond the family. Attachment theory examines one aspect of the relationship crucial to small infants but there are many other factors important in adult/child relationships.

There is little description of the relationship between carer and child which constantly constructs and negotiates meanings so that the child develops a sense of self and the broader culture in which the family live. There is little examination of how the dynamic of shared communication which expresses warmth, affection, humour, frequency of conflict as the child negotiates patterns of meaning is developed in significant relationships.

Dunn (1987) stated that two-year-old children show interest in other people in pretend play, in conversations with their mothers and siblings over stories and while watching television.

In *Young Children's Close Relationships* (1993) Dunn emphasised the importance of language and communication, cognition and perception for children in the development of social understanding and relationships. She also examines the significance of individual differences in temperament which make major contributions to the quality of relationships. These factors all have an impact on the child's capacity to make attachments which might not be evident in the laboratory setting of the Strange Situation research projects.

Clarke-Stewart (1988) stated that the Strange Situation does not have equivalent ecological validity for children looked after at home and those with extensive non-parental care, in that separations for those children are a part of everyday life. It is not appropriate to interpret behaviour in the Strange Situation as equivalent for children with such different case histories.

These children would have a different social construction of their relationship with their parents or carers and separations could have a different social meaning for them.

Harris (1994) observes that while children are sensitive to the particularities of the domestic environment they are also receptive to the pan-cultural concepts of intentionality, desire, belief. And while there are continuities in the attachments of children there are also major changes in the way they construct their ideas about the emotional states which underpin attachments. These changes occur through experience and understanding, but the nature of the emotionally charged experience within the home is likely to facilitate or impede the development of understanding.

Old Families – New Families

Some children are unable to live with their birth family. They may find new families and perhaps live 'nearly happily ever after'. Research by Tizard (1977) who made a study of late adoptions occurring around three to four years of age investigated their development and adjustment at aged eight. The children had been institutionalised more or less from birth. She discovered that nearly all the children had formed close attachments to their adoptive parents. The children were again seen at age 16 and the attachment to the adoptive family had been maintained.

This would question the idea that failure to form attachments at an early age is repeated throughout the life cycle. It is important to recognise that attachment relationships are relationships between two people and much depends on the quality of the carer to construct a responsive relationship with the child. The child who is fostered or adopted doesn't know the cultural rules of their new family and the ability to attach in this strange new environment relies on the adults' ability to explain how the family functions to the child. In these new and strange situations the child needs to be able to connect the past to the present.

Janet held on to her adoration of Elvis Presley as her link with the past. Her birth mother was a fan and later her foster carer had knitted her a cardigan with Elvis knitted into the pattern on the back and now in her adoptive placement, love of Elvis was her only link with a past littered with loss of parents, siblings, foster carers, social workers who had all come and gone from her life. Some days it was hard to remember her own name, or negotiate the new environment, so think of your favourite songs instead. 'Heartbreak Hotel,' 'All Shook Up', 'Crying in the Chapel' – sing the songs in your head to make the fear go away. Her new family understood how abandoned Janet felt as she shadowed them day and night, fearful that if she let them out of her sight they too would disappear, or she might get lost and never find her way back to her new home.

Some children do not find such an understanding family and drift on in the care system, bags packed, ready for moving on, as placements are sought or break down, and the children's stories express these confusions as they try to negotiate a meaning out of their circumstances.

Children's Stories of Separation and Loss

All the children whose stories follow express that sense of grief for the loss of their birth family and the fear that the new family will not accept them.

These are ever present themes in the stories of children who are trying to construct some meaning about what has happened to them. It is very difficult to settle in a new place, with new people, and be part of a family when everything that was familiar just disappears overnight. Rather like moving in with aliens on a strange planet, cut off from the roots of your existence.

Rachel

Rachel was eight when I met her. She had been adopted for two years and was the only child in the family. She had moved from a big town in the north of England to a country cottage in the west of England. She had been taken from her birth family as a baby, lived with foster carers, had an adoptive placement that broke down, and lived in a small children's home for two years before this adoptive placement.

Rachel loved her new parents but was angry and mistrustful. She had screaming rows with her mother and angry scenes with her father. All three acknowledged their own part in the way the family functioned. Mother fell into the 'victim' role with such ease that she became a choice target for Rachel's desire to control and Rachel and dad mirrored each other when they were angry.

Rachel said that sometimes living in the cottage felt uncomfortable, as though she didn't quite belong there. She wanted the time with me to narrate her life so far.

THE STORIES

We began our stories with a disaster. This is a common statement from children who have lost their sense of security and trust in the adult world.

Figure 5.1 Rachel trapped with rabbit

Figure 5.2 Trapped. Black anger in place where the hurt should be. Hurt in the gut

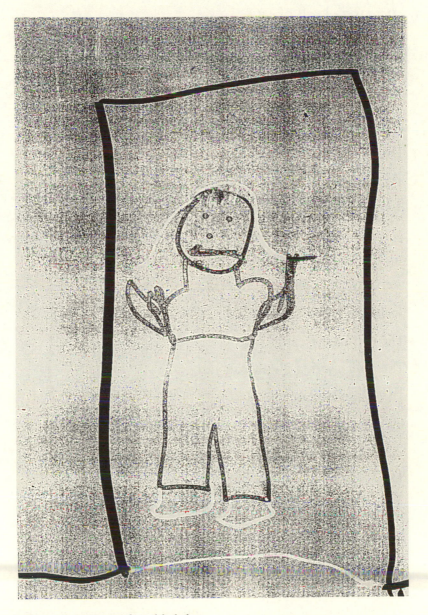

Figure 5.3 Trapped and helpless

The Crash

Once three cars had an accident.

There were loads of cars

Queuing up waiting.

And the police car came.

Three injured but not dead.

Eight children were injured but not badly hurt.

The youngest was seven.

The police car came.

It was so serious the army had to come out

The army came with a grappling iron but it went wrong and all the cars in the queue bashed into each other.

Lots of people died and the road was blocked for 4 hours.

There were two cars left.

The two racing cars

The police sorted all the cars out.

Three months later.

Everybody started to race including the policemen.

The army went back to the camp site.

The three racing cars as well.

Everybody got set to go and the winner was racing car no 23.

Everybody cheered except the policemen.

They didn't because they knew he was the one who set up the crash by putting a brick on the road.

And the splish splash was what started all the crashing in the first place.

These disaster stories are often structured by descriptions of numbers of people and objects as a way to control and give form to chaos and that constant impending feeling of doom lying just around the corner, so:

'Eight children were injured but not badly hurt,
The youngest was seven.'

Although in Rachel's story people were hurt they were 'not badly hurt' so things could have been worse, but maybe not. People died. Rachel couldn't decide. Was the disaster terrible or not so bad? But bad people seem to win the race at the end of the day.

Rachel put the toys away and chose a bag of family dolls. Children often relate a story then quickly finish as they feel their control slipping or they have tested the therapist's capacity to cope with disaster in the story. When children have assessed the therapist's capacity to cope with a general disaster story they often then relate a family story. Rachel told a family story with the dolls:

The Bungalow

This is a bungalow.

They have a sitting room, a bathroom, two bedrooms.

They live in the city.

They are posh.

They wear gowns.

They have a baby and a nanny to look after the baby.

They are kind to the baby.

Sometimes the grown ups fight.

They have a big Rover car in the back.

They have loads of money.

They have a granny who comes to stay in the family.

Gran stops in a hotel when she comes to stay.

The father is a doctor.

He is going to work.

He is in a good mood to-day.

Grandpa stays in the hotel.

This family live near the Queen and her family because they are so posh.

Grandma and grandpa have two granddaughters and two babies.

Grandma and grandpa are always moaning at the children.

'You should be grateful for what you've got'.

There is an older sister, 14, and a brother 12.

Mum works at the hairdresser.

It is very posh.

The nanny is a kind of sister and part of the family.

She has gone to work with the dad.

Rachel made another group.

There is a jail and there is a man who works at the jail.

Sometimes he is nasty because he has to be working in the jail.

There is a boy in bed who is six.

He is ill most of the time.

He has got flu.

They have a pig who lives in the bathroom and poos in the potty.

He is smelly.

A sheep sleeps in the bath with a turtle.

Back to the first group

The children have another toilet because they are so posh.

They are calm at the moment.

This was Rachel's exploration of this strange posh new family she had inherited. A mixture of reality and pretend, again focused on possessions, occupations as descriptions and a way to control the environment.

Feelings are expressed by blaming statements

'you should be grateful'

Then the other family, shameful because they are a 'smelly' family who live near the prison.

Rachel wanted to tell her story to her parents at the end of our meeting and was pleased when they listened and responded, especially to the bit about gran. It is gran who says:

'you should be grateful'

and that bit was very like dad's mum and the family groaned together. A moment of attachment for Rachel.

At the beginning of the next session, Rachel drew a picture of her teddy bear. She pours out all her thoughts to Fred when she is sad. She narrated her picture to me:

Fred

This is a picture of a teddy bear.

He belongs to Rachel and his name is Fred.

He has two parents – a mum and a dad.

They adopted him when he was little.

His real mum can't look after him.

He is cute.

Sometimes he has temper tantrums and he gets very very angry.

He says 'I hate you' to his mum and dad

Sometimes he calls to Emma because his mum was Emma.

Sometimes he calls to Rachel, 'Rachel.'

He calls Rachel Emma when they talk together.

He has a longing for his real mum but he can't even remember her.

He wants to love Rachel but he is not sure how.

So this week he is going to try and say 'I love you' to Rachel five times and mean it.

This is an experiment.

Rachel really wanted to show she loved her new parents and we worked out ways she could do this by sharing her feelings with them as well as with Fred. She still felt a great resistance and a sense that she was being disloyal to a birth mother she couldn't even remember. And anyway there were all those other mothers in between and nasty fathers, then no fathers then this one with a temper so like hers. It was hard to separate the people from the role of parent.

In the following sessions Rachel began to explore ideas about herself. After all, how can you have a relationship with these parents if you don't know who you are at all? In one session she drew a picture of herself and made this narrative.

'A smily/happy mouth.

She could eat people when she is angry.

Her top is green, both nice and cross.

She has a rude cheeky tongue that says bad things.

She has a snotty nose.

Her hair is happy.

Her eyes are kind.

Inside her she is scared of lots of things.

What things?

In case she is thrown out of the house.

What else?

That she won't have any friends.

Are there any other feelings?

Only a tiny bit of nice feeling.

What?

She is going to try harder to fit into the family.

How?

Maybe she can say a few nice things.

Tell me about the legs

The legs are full of anger.

What about?

About how unfair everything has been.

For example?

Not staying in one place.

Keep on moving.

Angry with her mum who she can't even remember.

Yet loving her as well.

Angry with her adoptive mum for not being her real mum.

Angry when she went away on holiday.

Angry that she'll throw me out.

So I get bad tempered so she will throw me out quickly.

What about the feet?

The feet are happy feet, dancing feet.

If only all the body was a dancing body

Then life would be better for everyone.

Has she got arms?

She has got arms

What are they like?

They are horrible arms.

Why?

The arms are helpless.

Crying for help.

Wanting to love but don't know how.

The arms are coming out of the tummy so can't do much about this.

What about the ears?

Ears are big.

Why?

They listen to what other people are saying about me.

They are listening for good things.

They are also listening to hear

'We are fed up with her.

Let's kick her out.'

Rachel told the story of her picture in the third person so she was able to distance herself from the girl in the picture who was herself but not herself as it was the story of a picture.

Rachel drew another picture of herself. She was trapped and paralysed. She described it like this.

Rachel is in a building, not sure what.

She is trapped.

Two huge brick walls on either side.

A wall above the head.

A very tiny hole to breathe

And the hot sun outside which makes the walls unbearably hot

She is alone with her pet rabbit,

He is suffering.

The anger in the chest.

Is about not being loved.

By Mum.

The mum before.

The people before who wanted to adopt her but didn't.

This is a cage floating on the sea.

Birds fly about.

And the golden bird can bite holes in the cage and rescue Rachel.

Her heart is in the stomach.

Hate is where the heart should be.

This image described Rachel's dilemma. She really was stuck in a kind of cage and she was very aware of the loss of love in her heart and everything misplaced in her body. There were many stories about this sense of helplessness and also the fluttering golden bird who might be able to warm her heart and set her free. Could she realign her body and drag her heart out of her stomach?

Her communication with her parents improved slowly, but some weeks anger flared up, especially between dad and Rachel. There was a greater acceptance by her parents of the difficulties of building trust when the past had been so precarious. All three were more aware of their individual flash points. Life has its ups and downs.

Rachel defined her self/environment through a drawing and a narrative.

She talked as she drew.

The Haunted House

The house belongs to Rachel.

It's a mixture of scary and nice.

The spare room is where monsters hang out.

Such terrible monsters that nobody knows what they are like but they draw on the walls and make a terrible mess.

Ooze comes out of that room.

This is the dining room.

Where good ghosts hang out.

They try to get rid of the bad ghosts.

The living room is the place where nobody hangs out.

It is dirty with spiders' webs.

They think that room is very very haunted because of the spiders' webs.

Rachel dabbed coloured spots over the drawing.

One day they find that the house is spotty.

It means that the bad monsters have gone away.

I asked who lived in the house.

The people in the house is Rachel, just Rachel.

One day Rachel finds the leader Ann in the living room in the haunted house which means somebody has been in there for years.

They have been trying to make it tidy and they have succeeded.

Just enough tidy.

Then the house looks like this.

The monsters at the top of the house have gone.

The good monsters have gone as well.

Rachel is left.

Then suddenly all the spots in the house have gone except one on the chimney.

There is nice clean wallpaper, bright blue.

It's a safer place.

Then all the house is covered in blue wallpaper.

It's goodish/bad because they find two more monsters in the garden.

The two monsters left letters in the garden saying good-bye we won't bother you again.

The End.

This was one of our last stories together. Rachel had done a little tidying, the best she could do for the moment, but it was safer. The monsters had gone but there was a lot of ooze still around which could attract the monsters back.

We thought this was a reasonable appraisal of the changes that had taken place for Rachel and her parents.

She wanted to love and be loved but was also very resistant to the idea. How could you trust people? It was too soon for her to believe she was loveable so she still got angry with her parents. This was exhausting for them as they had to cope with her anger and her tantrums. It is difficult not to get engulfed by the anger and feel as sad as Rachel and disregard her self-awareness and sensitivity.

Rachel felt her emotions were all in the wrong places but there is hope in those happy feet. Maybe they can kick the heart into place. Keep the feet dancing Rachel!

Abigail

Abigail was eight and was to be adopted. She was having trouble understanding the rules in her new family and anyway she wanted to rule the world. She had experienced neglect and abuse from her birth family and felt bad about herself. She had frightening night-mares when monsters came and abused her.

Her first story was about a monster. Not the dream monster but the shameful Abigail monster.

Disgusting Monster

There was once a monster called Disgusting.

He ate slime and farted and he was a monster.

He shouted a lot at people.

Wanted his own way all the time.

People thought he was a monster but they still loved him.

He lived with his mum who was very nasty to him because he was so naughty to her because he wanted his own way all the time.

As his mum got *her* own way all the time he thought it was OK to get *his* own way.

He was given the slime by a girl called Sarah because she wanted him to get into trouble.

When he got into trouble she just laughed.

This clearly was a statement of Abigail's position; her feelings of loathing about herself, her desire to be in charge and take the parenting role and the problems with her peers and the spitefulness of Sarah which also existed in Abigail. First narratives are often world statements and Abigail wanted to rule her world.

Abigail and I talked about the role of mothers and daughters and we had the same conversation with her mother at the end of the session. Abigail wanted to understand the boundaries in the family and her mother wanted her care and love to be acknowledged and respected.

They made some rules to get on better with each other, clarifying the responsibilities of parent and child.

In the following sessions Abigail continued to construct a social world for herself, integrating past and present. She told me a robber story.

The Robber

The robber farted.

He was very naughty.

He wanted to rule the world.

The robber had a really bad mum.

He had a little house

But as he grew up he didn't have money.

So he robbed and farted all the time

Because he had no mum to help him

And tell him what was right.

Then back to that nasty girl Sarah.

Sarah

A girl called Sarah gave the monster some yellow slime

And he shot it through his bottom.

He was sick through his nose and his mouth

And he got into lots of trouble.

   'Served himself right' said Sarah.

She was glad that he got into trouble by his mum.

Sarah was a bit of a nasty girl.

After the stories we talked a little about school and rules about making friends. Not being bossy, not becoming like Sarah. Getting advice from mum. In the next session, Abigail spoke of her scary dreams and made this story.

The Scary Dream

In this dream monsters came.

They want to catch the children and eat them.

The monsters are men and ladies and they show their willies

And fart

And the ladies show their breasts and bottoms.

The children hide behind a rock.

The grown ups say

   'Come here little children'

They have to go over there and they will be turned into frogs.

They turn them into toads and they eat them for dinner.

Tonight the children don't get turned into frogs because they turn themselves into wrestlers and beat the monsters up.

They run away and shout 'help'.

And when they wake up the nice mum and dad are there to look after them.

We had explored strategies to cope with dream monsters. I suggested Abigail turned herself into Supergirl and fly away from the monsters but she preferred to become a wrestler who ran away when things got nasty. Better than being turned into a frog. The scary stories continued.

The Haunted House

This is my house.

It is haunted by ghosts.

They knock the furniture down and they don't put it back up.

They frighten the people who live there especially the children.

They made ghost noises which made their dreams twice as scary.

They can't get rid of the ghosts.

They have to put up with them.

The children could ignore the ghosts,

Or talk about the dream

Or get the doctor to give them something to make them sleep.

The children do nice things for their parents.

They love the mum and dad

But sometimes they are bossy with dad because he gets them ready for school.

They don't want to go to school but stay at home.

After this story, the family helped Abigail change the furniture in her bedroom to make the room safer for her at night. She had her mattress on the floor for a while so there was no room under the bed for 'monsters'. More sleep and mornings, the time with dad before school got better.

Abigail told two stories, one in a world without parents, and one about a family. She was able to express negative feelings and test out if she was still accepted.

The Tricky Pink Power Ranger and the Mermaids

The Pink Power Ranger and Abigail live at the bottom of the sea together.

They have no parents so they boss people about.

They swear and scream and shout.

Then the Green Power Ranger comes and punches Pink Power Ranger and Abigail until they die.

He has to save the world and does a very good job of it.

After they die the Green Power Ranger took over the world and was very good.

He was nice to the people and stopped monsters coming.

One day a dragon came and cuts Ann's face.

The Family

Mum, dad Abigail the baby and granny are out in the daytime together.

Another granny is bashing the granny.

Dad is being a bit bossy.

They like him but not when he is bossy.

Everybody likes it in the family.

One day the girl goes out and got lost.

Her sister Abigail organises a search party.

The mum and dad were crying their eyes out.

They couldn't help it.

A witch came into the family one day and made a lot of noise and went away.

Nobody else got lost and they all lived happily ever after.

Abigail looked after the sisters because the parents had to go out most of the time.

At the end of the stories I acknowledged my cut face and my witch-like characteristics expressed in the stories. The world without parents seemed violent and unsafe and the Green Power Ranger couldn't stop the dragon in the end. The parents in the family story still could not find the lost girl, Abigail had to do that. We acknowledged that it takes a long time to trust the capabilities of adults if you have been let down and assaulted by them. It is also very hard to let go of being the boss in the family.

Family life got better, Mum took charge more and coped with the shouting and bossiness. Both parents felt affirmed as parents and Abigail was able to say how she loved them. Her last story described her social world and her strategies for coping with being a child of the Oddies.

The Oddie Family

This is Miss Oddie but she is married.

She lives with Mr Oddie who is called Steve and Ms Oddie is called Susan.

They had four children but they are grown up.

They were good parents and looked after the children very well.

The have two grandchildren – a girl and a boy

They are like angels because they never fight.

The dad is a OK dad.

The mum is an OK mum.

Their children are kind and the grandchildren are kind.

Why are they called Oddie?

They are odd because they have a golden nose, yellow cheeks and everything else is OK

They have funny voices that sweep up and down and everybody goes

'Oh, ho, nasty voices, nasty voices.'

They just walk away when people say nasty things.

They have been alive for 100 years which is very odd.

They will live for ever and they want to live for ever.

The children and grandchildren also want to live for ever.

All the family have pink and white bedrooms.

Margaret

Margaret was nine when I saw her. She was long-term fostered with a family in London. She came from the north of England.

Margaret had experienced extreme physical violence from her birth father and was taken into care. One adoptive placement had broken down because of abuse by a carer and Margaret had been in her present placement for over a year. She was loved and wanted in the family but she expected to be rejected again. Margaret loved making stories and she loved just to play. At our first meeting she started a story immediately.

The Mermaid World

In the mermaid world live three mermaids.

And a giant rat who wanted to kill the mermaids.

They were scared of the rat and hid behind their leader called Ariel.

The rat was angry and was specially angry with Ariel.

They had some friends who were fiercer that the rat.

The dragon and the sea monster who protected them.

In the end the dragon and the dinosaur saved the mermaids and the rat died of fright.

After the story Margaret began to talk about what she would do if the family threw her out. She said she would run back into the house and grab some food from the fridge so that when she was on the streets she wouldn't starve. I asked Margaret why she thought she would be thrown out and she said it was just a fear. We talked about what you do if you are alone as a child on the street. You go to the police who will call Social Services. This was explored with a lot of 'Yes but, what if' and we solved all the puzzles together.

I said it might be a good idea to talk to her mum about these fears and she did, and was reassured, although the feelings still surge up from time to time. Margaret had a story ready at our second meeting:

This is Zarlov from an alien planet. She came to earth to
live in Hanworth. She had 3 arms on the planet so one
disappeared when she went to earth.

Figure 5.4 Margaret's drawing of Zarlov who comes from another planet

Figure 5.5 The story of my life. Drowned in a snow storm

The Little Town

Ghosts live there and it is very scary.

5,002 ghosts live there and it is called the Ghost Town.

A witch came to the ghost town and struck Ann with her fingernail and Ann's leg turned green and fell off

And Ann became a ghost by the evil touch of the witch woman.

Now there are 5,003 ghosts.

The job of the ghosts is to scare all human people who come to the town.

The next person who came to the town was a princess and she brought her mother and the prince.

There were four ghost babies in the town.

The princess and the prince and the queen felt a bit sad to see babies as ghosts.

The witch is the boss of Ghost Town.

She isn't really a person.

She's a huge giant so big that all anyone can see of Ghost Town is her finger walking through the street.

> *Margaret put a toy witch's finger on her finger and walked her finger through the toys.*

Sometimes she puts a speed on her fingers and makes them dance.

The people are scared when they see the fingers and sometimes the ghosts are scared because she can punish them.

She can turn humans into ghosts or ghosts into hurting fingers that can hit children.

They hit everybody but definitely children.

The Prince and Princess ran out of Ghost Town.

Back to the park and told their dad who went to Ghost Town and destroyed all those houses.

Not the trees.

And the dinosaur stayed alone in the forest.

Margaret then changed the small toys from the Ghost Town to make a forest and told this story.

Chapter 2 The Forest

This is a good and a bad place.

There are trees but some of the ghost fingers are still lying there standing upright.

But they are dead.

One day they disappeared into thin air and nobody knows what happened to them except they are dead and just blew up.

In the first story Margaret wanted me to experience the pain and suffering of living in Ghost Town while the princess was in the end helped to the forest by her father. Margaret had an image of the forest as a safer place even though the ghost fingers were still there until they blew up. It was important for her to narrate a father who cared for children, as she found it unbearable to contemplate the violence of her birth father's attack on her. After the story Margaret recited this rhyme.

Johnny on the railroad picking up stones,
along came the engine and broke Johnny's bones,
O said Johnny, that's not fair,
O said the driver, I don't care.

The hate and violence in nursery rhymes was a favourite way of Margaret to express anger about her past.

Jack and Guy
Went out in the Rye
And they found a little boy

With one black eye
'Come' says Jack 'let's knock him
On the head'
'No' says Guy
'Let's buy him some bread
You buy one loaf
And I'll buy two
And we'll bring him up
As other folk do.'

We looked at the illustrations in Maurice Sendak's book illustrating two nursery rhymes *We Are All In The Dumps with Jack and Guy* (1993). All those abandoned children in the end finding a slightly better place, being brought up

'As other folks do'

Margaret began a period of frantic writing of stories in her spare time as though a huge creative force had been released. She made little books, diaries, story books, with paper I gave her. She scribbled away making her own private stories. Some of the fear and dread is put into this writing. She keeps the stories private and says she feels more rested. But she still thinks about being abandoned or running away. We go on together.

Rachel, Abigail and Margaret

Rachel, Abigail and Margaret all expressed fear of abandonment and fear of making new attachments. They all felt slightly uncomfortable in their new homes as if they didn't quite fit in. The wider environment was confusing. What would happen if they were abandoned or got lost on the street? How would they find their way back home? They were not clear where their old homes were and whether they were now in England or a foreign country.

They felt a great searing loss for their birth parents, however much they had hurt them, even when they had only a slight memory of them. They were often angry with their adoptive parents for not being their birth parents.

Rachel and Abigail wanted to be the parents and control the action, Margaret had a great desire at times to run away and be on her own. They all had considerable insight but found it difficult to put self-awareness into action to make things better for themselves. When I think of them on their journey to find a coherent self I recall the poem by e.e. cummings.

maggie and milly and molly and may

maggie and milly and molly and may
went down to the beach (to play one day)

and maggie discovered a shell that sang
so sweetly she couldn't remember her troubles, and

milly befriended a stranded star
whose rays five languid fingers were;

and molly was chased by a horrible thing
which raced sideways while blowing bubbles: and

may came home with a smooth round stone
as small as a world and as large as alone.

For whatever we lose (like a you or a me)
it's always ourselves we find in the sea

Andrew

Andrew was seven when I first met him. He had been in care for some years because his mother was a crack cocaine user and unable to care for him. He had been through three foster placements and in the third he had been consistently sexually abused by an uncle who lived with the family.

I first saw Andrew at that time. He then went to an adoptive placement which broke down very quickly and is now with a foster carer who has given him a loving and caring experience of family life.

For the first year of therapy Andrew was very angry and tried to control all our sessions. Sometimes he would play and tell stories,

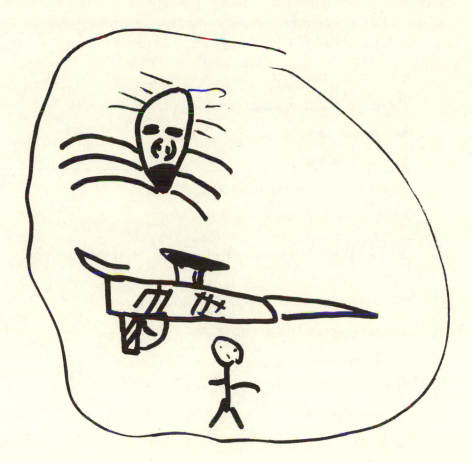

The monster is called Spider Man. He is killed by a
bazooka which belongs to Stick Man. When he is dead
Stick man eats him. They live in a cave and Andrew is safe
because he is out of the cave. Stick man can't get out of
the cave so Andrew is safe.

Figure 5.6 Andrew keeping control of monsters

other times he refused to do anything at all. His life was full of pain and loss. The appearances and disappearances of his birth mother were unbearable. Her greed for drugs was monstrous to him.

Mrs Disgusting Idiot

There was once a monster called Mrs Disgusting Idiot.

And she ate slime all day and all night.

All winter and all summer.

All the time in the whole wide world.

And it made her sad.

Then all those other monsters he had met and were perhaps now part of him.

There was another monster called Mr Idiot

And he ate gooey slime

And it punched out of his head

And made rude burping noises.

He was disgusting.

He couldn't control his body.

There was a fighting bastard monster.

He put all slime about his face

And other people's faces

Even though they didn't want it.

He ate so much he shouted and growled.

He ate people.

He ate other monsters, children, grown-ups

He crunched them to death in his jaws.

They screamed.

Andrew's world at this time was catastrophic. He described it with small toys in a sand tray.

The Evil World

This is an evil world ruled by the dragon.

There is a dead man called Captain Scarlet

Who the dragon has killed.

The car is looking for the man.

The land in this country is rough and bumpy.

The dragon just sits and eats people.

And the car just searches for the lost men.

He found Captain Scarlet but it's too late,

He is dead.

The dragon is lying on his side

Because he wants to watch things.

The dragon is covering the sand.

Then he sits on it.

He is the king of the World.

Captain Scarlet dies again in the sinking sand.

There are army people who came to shoot the dragon.

Now the dragon is dead

And there is nobody left in the world.

It is hopeless.

The dragon is buried and the land has gone for ever.

Does anybody come alive again?

The dragon does come alive again

But it is another world.

The new world is sort of scary.

There is a dragon and three knights.

They are trying to kill the dragon

But it's a dinosaur world.

There are crazy people as well.

It's a good and a bad world.

> *Andrew placed all the toys on the sand tray so the sand was no longer visible.*

It's really scary and horrible and fierce to live there.

This world is very crowded.

There are no families.

Just crowds.

Nobody cares for anybody else.

Nobody trusts anybody.

Everybody has to fight for themselves.

There are no good or bad people.

Everybody is just scared

Except the knights and the armies.

Because they are cruel and vicious.

Andrew moved to his present placement and was able to express his anger about his failed adoption with this story.

Once upon a time there was a super idiot called Super Idiot

And he did very nasty things to Bart Simpson.

Then Bart Simpson got his super weapon ready

And got on his skateboard and he flew away.

He knocked out Super Idiot.

Then went after crazy mum who was out of her head.

Bart Simpson was in a very angry mood.

He got on his skateboard and attacked everybody.

Super Bart came to the rescue of everybody.

But Bart Simpson fell and died.

Super Bart killed Bad Bart.

Then Good Bart came alive and did flips on his skateboard.

Andrew came for many sessions and refused to play. He expressed his anger through silence, making rude comments, but he kept the rules of no hitting and hurting. We went on together. Each session was a small battle of wits as he would think of thing to do to irritate: open all the drawers in the desk, open the cupboard, lean out of the window, refuse to play, hide toys in his pocket and refuse to give them back until I insisted. We were both drained as the sessions ended.

Then one day he drew a mask and narrated this story.

The Mask

The mask is called Tom.

'You don't like me' said the mask.

   'Shall we be friends?'

   'What shall we do?'

Yes just pull faces.

Green for slimy stuff.

Yellow for the eyes.

This is a sneaky colour.

The red is for nastiness.

Andrew smeared the mask with slime

Even if we get the slime off

Tom is still nasty.

The next session Andrew wanted to paint another mask.

This is M-ask.

It is a he.

He is really called M-arse.

He is nice but he is also an arse hole.

Andrew told me not to write.

I asked why.

He told me to write,

'Andrew doesn't want me to write anything.

Because he is nothing.'

At the next session I was told that Andrew's mother was in prison. I told Andrew and for the first time there was a feeling of trust between us. I had told him the truth not avoided it. He cried. He was worried that his mother would only get bread and water. I reassured him. We sat together. No need for talk or play.

In the next session Andrew told me this story with the toys.

The Sad Country

This is a sad country.

The dad is dead

And there are only cars and men

And women and Power Rangers.

There are sharks and dolphins

And Andrew always wants more.

There is never enough.

He is greedy and want to control everything.

Andrew asked me to tell the next bit of the story

Andrew wants to control everything.

Not keep the rules.

Not make stories.

Just make mess.

He said that his world in the sand tray is chaos.

Andrew continued:

Nobody standing up.

Everybody hurt.

It's a mess.

But sometimes people stand up

But not for very long.

They all ended up lying down.

Drugged out of their minds on crack cocaine.

Andrew was doing well at school and feeling loved in his foster family. He told me that he wanted to be adopted now because he knew that his mother couldn't look after him and he wanted to have parents to care for him.

He made up this story:

The Lost Scary Monster

There was once a lost scary monster

Who lived in a big big cave.

He didn't know who he was so he's called Dopey.

But Ann knows this monster well and thinks he is good.

Except when he gobs slime and sticks it all over his face.

The world becomes a little less chaotic.

The Power Rangers World

The Power Rangers in this world are quite small.

There is a car in this world, stuck in a cage,

But it escaped and the cage was empty.

The Power Rangers climbed to the top of the sand dune.

Then they got stuck in the van.

They tried to get out but they couldn't.

In the end they got out and came racing down the dune

Collecting all the sand.

The country has a huge hill at one end and then a big pile of sand everywhere.

It is a desert.

With a little lake.

Andrew has begun to evaluate his experiences of care. He has had some really warm experiences of foster care and some horrible ones as well. His present placement is safe and loving but he wants a family who will own and adopt him. His world is still barren and he has frightening experiences of carers and parents who exposed him to various forms of sexual abuse.

He is beginning to unlock those terrors. It's hazardous journey. We go on.

Lost in Care

The final three stories are from two children who still drift in the care system.

Figure 5.7 Angus the compliant child waiting to move on

Angus

Angus has learning difficulties and has moved from adoptive placements to foster placements to a small specialist units back to foster carers.

I have seen him on and off since he was eight. He is now 13.

He told me the first story when he was 11 waiting to go to a specialist unit. He drew a picture on the back of my blue mat and narrated this story.

Bart Simpson in the Forest

This is a golden forest.

Called Forest Gump.

Bart Simpson went into the magic forest called Forest Gump.

Bart Simpson felt bad about himself.

So he went into the magic forest and saw a magic tree.

If you touch the magic tree you get powers and wishes.

The magic tree was beautiful and Bart Simpson gasped with amazement when he saw it.

The dragon comes to the forest and brings fire.

This is a bad thing.

In The Forest. Part 2.

For a minute I thought I was home.

One day a genie came to the forest.

He was good and gave people wishes.

He gave Bart Simpson seven wishes.

Bart said:

I wish I could have a family.

I wish I could have everything in the world.

I wish I could have Ann.

I wish I could have a motor bike.

I wish I could have my own house.

I wish I could have the genie.

I wish I could have a parrot.

And all his wishes came true.

Figure 5.8 The crazy family

I saw Angus again after he had moved from the Unit to a foster placement which was clearly not appropriate. Angus was 13.

Bart Simpson was last seen in the land of Forest Gump,

An enchanted forest.

He thought the dragon might save him.

He got out of the forest and went on a journey to the land of thicko Nerds.

It was chaos there.

Everyone went crazy.

Bart Simpson was always on the move.

So he had a suitcase ready packed in case he had to move on.

He had to move on because he was stupid.

Sometimes he laughed like a two-year-old.

He got bad tempered, misbehaved so people wouldn't like him.

I told Angus a story of the revels on The Gump at St Just in Cornwall.

The Old Man On The Gump

There is a hill at St Justin in Cornwall called the Gump which is supposed to be a meeting place for the little people who have often been seen there enjoying themselves with music, drinking and dancing.

The little people don't usually like intruders but well mannered onlookers were welcomed and sometimes they were given small but precious gifts.

There was an old man from St Just who had heard a lot about the treasures of the little people and one night decided to get some for himself.

He began to climb up the Gump and soon heard music under his feet although he could see nothing.

Suddenly the hill opened up and before his eyes a stream of little people poured out of the side of the hill with musicians, soldiers and a hideous band of Spriggans who were the guardians of the Gump and the treasure.

The little people set up fine tables on the hillside covered with brilliant gem-encrusted gold and silverware.

The whole hillside was lit up with thousands and thousands of jewels twinkling from every blade of grass.

The old man was astonished by the wonder of it all.

Then the court appeared led by the prince and princess who moved to the high table which was the most magnificent bejewelled and dazzling table.

Well, thought the old man, if I could only crawl to the prince's table I should have a catch sure enough and be a rich man for life.

As he crept forward he did not realise that the Spriggans had thrown little strings around him and that they still held the ends of the threads.

He crawled to the table and discovered that all was dark and gloomy behind him but the mound was a blaze of light.

As he got closer he saw that every one of the thousands of eyes of the little people was fixed on him.

Then everything became dark around him.

He was jerked sharply on his back.

Every limb from head to foot was as if stuck full of pins and pinched with tweezers.

He could not move.

He lay on his back with his arms outstretched at the bottom of the Gump.

One little Spriggan jumped all over his face with great delight until he laughed and shouted

'Away, away, I smell the day.'

At length the sun arose and he found he had been tied to the ground by gossamer spider's webs now covered with dew and glistening like diamonds in the sunshine.

He shook himself and was free...

Angus thought it was a bit like his life. Forever grasping for jewels which vanished in the daylight, like gossamer.

Carol

Carol has been in care for two years. She is eleven and is waiting for a long-term foster placement.

There was once a girl called Vicki

Who felt that her life was like a pile of pink slime.

It had no shape, ran all over the place had jelly inside and could be pulled apart very easily.

A stretch of continuous slime but pulled apart too easily.

So who was going to give this life some shape?

Perhaps if somebody cared for you they could stop the slime spreading all over the place.

She put all the mess in a pile and gave it shape so it was no longer a pile of slime

But the shape of a well known life.

'Sad Songs and Gay'

These children are coping with difficult life events. They are adaptable and even perfect families need to be adaptable. Read the Ukranian story of *Sad Songs and Gay*

Sad Songs and Gay

Once upon a time, there lived a man and his wife who had a whole houseful of children but only enough land for a rabbit to hop over. They worked day and night, all of them, just to keep body and soul together, but loved songs and were always singing.

Some time passed, and the wife died. This was a terrible blow to the man and his children, and only sad songs now sounded in the house.

Not far from them lived a great lord. One day he came to their home, put a purse stuffed with money on a bench and asked the man how many children he had.

'Ten' the man replied.

'Isn't that too many for a palace like yours?' the lord said. 'Let me have one of your children and you can take the purse.'

The man called his children.

'The lord has offered me a purse full of money in return for one of you,' he said. 'Does anyone want to go with him? The one who does will eat white buns and sleep on feathered beds.'

The children burst out crying.

'No one want to go with you, sir' said the man.

The lord thought it over.

'Oh well, it's up to you, but your songs keep me awake, so I'll let you have the money if you stop them singing.'

'So be it' the man agreed.

He took the money and the lord went away.

For a time silence reigned in the house. But one day one of the boys suddenly began singing. and so sad was his song that the tears showed in his brothers' and sisters' eyes.

The poor man took the lord's purse and hurried to him with it.

> 'I'm sorry, sir, but neither my children nor my songs are for sale.'

And from that day the poor man's house rang with songs, sad ones and gay.

And his children may still be singing away today if they hadn't all died of hunger.

CHAPTER 6

Stories of Heroes, Wishes and Dreams

Why Did The Peacock Scream?

why did the peacock scream?
    in order to hear himself.
why did the peacock scream?
    because he couldn't see himself.

R.D. Laing

The Ubiquitous One

On leaving the city of Stravasti, the Buddha had to cross an extensive plain. From their various heavens, the gods threw him parasols to cover him from the sun. In order to avoid giving offence or slighting any of his benefactors, the Buddha courteously multiplied himself, and thus each one of the gods beheld a Buddha who walked along with his own parasol

Moriz Winternitz, *Geschichte der indischen literatur* (1920)

The Dream of Chuang Tzu

Chuang Tzu dreamt he was a butterfly and, when he awoke, did not know if he was a man who had dreamt he was a butterfly or a butterfly who was dreaming he was a man.

Chiang Tzu (1889)

Constructing a Hopeful Story

How to be a person rather than a label? Those dreaded labels — abused, conduct disordered, attachment disordered — often seem to be placed on an object rather than a person. And often children are blamed for their histories and they accept the blame and the shame. So how is it possible to develop an identity which contains the past but narrates an extended self beyond those labels? Not always having to scream like the peacock, but able to find stories which, like the Buddha, can fit under many parasols.

The relationship between child and therapist can start the narration of more heroic and hopeful stories if there is respect for the child as an individual.

Rachel, Abigail and Margaret, described in the last chapter, experienced many of the same anxieties but they were unique individuals not baggages of symptoms and the solutions they made were personal, determined by their social environment as well as their personal temperaments. We worked hard together, not forcing the pace but not being sentimental. Baudrillard (1993) states:

> Only therapy makes madness obscene… It is what drowns the cruelty of evil in the sentimentality of the gaze that is obscene. What is supremely obscene is pity, indecent condescension.

The Consolation of a Story

One of the most important functions of a story or folk tale is the sense of hope and consolation it can bring. Tolkien (1966) defined four factors which give power to folk and fairy stories: fantasy, recovery, escape and consolation. He considered that by moving to another world the fairy tale enables the reader to regain a clear view of their situations. The placing of objects from our everyday world in a luminous, estranged setting compels us to perceive and cherish them in a new way, to see new connections between past and present.

While such stories may be an 'escape', Tolkien argues that escape is not cowardly but can be heroic. 'Why should man be scorned if, finding himself in prison, he tries to get out and go home?' (p.60). The escape can be liberating if we can accept its consolation.

Bloch (1930) also stated that the fairy tale narrates a wish-fulfilment which is not bound by it own time and the apparel of its contents. The young protagonist who sets out to find happiness is still around, as strong as ever; so is the dreamer who is caught up with the girl of his dreams and with the distant secure home.

The Role of the Hero

In his book *The Morphology of the Folktale* (1968) Propp describes two kinds of heroes. If the hero goes off in search of, for example, the kidnapped girl, and the story follows the search, then he, not the kidnapped girl is the hero of the tale. Heroes of this type are termed *seekers*. The second kind of hero emerges in a story when a young boy or girl is driven out or seized and the thread of the narrative is linked to his or her fate. Then the hero of the tale is the seized or banished boy or girl. There are no seekers in such tales. Heroes of this sort are called *victimised heroes*.

Teneze (1970) states that the hero lacks something and goes in search for aid (intermediaries) to achieve happiness. The structure of every magic folk tale conforms to this quest. In these folk narratives and fairy stories trials and tribulations are the province of heroes.

It can be helpful for the child in therapy to reframe their experiences through their own storymaking, which defines trials and tribulations as the human condition and the protagonist as heroic. This would seem an extended identity from that of a psychological/psychiatric label or to be endlessly portrayed as the victim rather than the victimised hero on a hopeful quest for honour and the safety of home, however that can be defined.

The Stories

Natasha's Hero: The Giant Detector

Natasha is long-term fostered, living with her carer (whom she calls mother) and another foster child three years older. These two define themselves as sisters. Her birth mother is Irish and her birth father is probably African. She first came to her foster family when she was eight and has now been there for five years. Initially, we spent much time together, making some sense of her early years and thinking about the neglect and abuse she experienced with her birth mother and later in care.

Natasha disclosed sexual abuse early in her present placement and many angry exchanges followed between the carer and social services and some wounds are hard to heal. It is a long and lonely battle to have the abuse of a child in the care system acknowledged in a way which is healing.

I now see Natasha when she asks to see me and she phones to make her appointments. Sometimes this is because there are incidents at home or school; sometimes it's just to meet. Natasha wants to think about her origins, the meaning of family, and her determination to live an interesting and fulfilling life. Natasha always likes to draw and make stories. She is lively, has a sly sense of humour, a hero of her own life.

Her first two narrations are about families: black and white families in England and a black family in Africa. The first narration defines membership of the family, the second the departure of a member of the family who doesn't want to go but it is the custom. There are no resolutions to these narrations, just statements about family members; the tentative beginnings of a folk tale.

This is a naked woman. She is on the metal fence and the beast is weeing in her mouth.

It is a prickly metal fence. She is tied up on it and then he puts his willy in her mouth.

Figure 6.1 A picture Natasha drew of herself aged 8

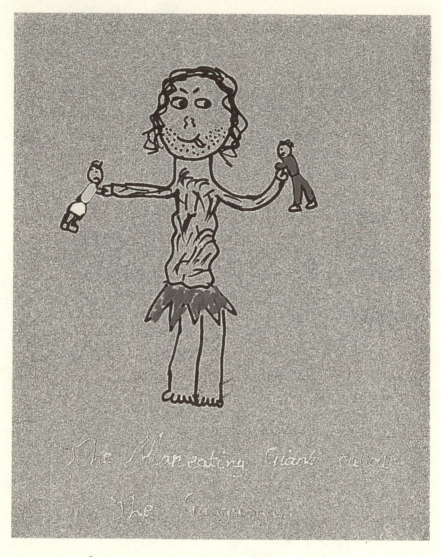

Figure 6.2 The Monster Guagwoga

Figure 6.3 Nathasha in heroic mode

The Black and White Families

There was once a mother and a baby and a daddy.

A black daddy and a white mummy and a black mummy and a white daddy.

They lived at 120 Gorgonville but although it sounds horrible it was nice.

This family liked living at Gorgonville and the children went to school and the two mums talked to each other.

The black and the white mum.

The black mum was called Geesha and the white mum Alba.

They liked the children and the children were happy.

Alba and Geesha's husbands were brothers.

Alba had two children and Geesha one.

The African Family

Teresa live in Africa and she was separated from her family and sent to America.

There was a war and famine in Africa so she escaped but she left behind all her family.

And she was alone.

It was a tradition to go because her parents couldn't look after her because they were very poor.

But her mother had not really loved her because she was from her mum's first marriage.

Mum had been married eight times and she had eight children and she loved Teresa a tiny little bit.

Mum liked her the least.

Her mother loved Surumba her littlest brother born recently.

Teresa was angry about that.

But she was loved by her father who had no custody over her.

The End.

These were Natasha's longings and yearnings about her family and a fictional account of the feelings of rejection she has experienced. She worried about a father so we invented a heroic father together. Sometimes he was African, sometimes living in the Caribbean like her present mother's family. We invented enough fathers to satisfy Natasha.

She then told me a Power Rangers story. This is a proper story. There is a hero who is called in to mend the exhausted, possibly drunken, Green Power Ranger. I am pleased to note that Ann (the hero for once), got a reward for her efforts.

The Crazy Power Ranger

It involves Tommy and Zak – he is black, black.

They are in Bobbleville which is a nice place.

Full of fun and exciting things like the park.

One day they were walking along and Tommy's mum was talking to Jennifer.

They had found Tommy, the Green Power Ranger, lying on the ground.

He had fainted because he was tired and he'd done too much fighting.

He was saying 'Go, Go, Power Rangers'.

Then he went funny as though severely drunk.

He was zapped by the wicked queen Nita.

So Tommy's mum called Ann.

She got her children to pick him up and put him in the car.

They had to share a seat because there were too many in the car.

They took Tommy to the Park Hospital

And they put him in the sun to dry.

When he woke up he was vicious so they put him in a cage.

They came back from the hospital to the park.

And they all played while the Green Power Ranger dried out.

Nobody else got drunk.

It was a kind of reasonable day.

But they wouldn't want to meet the Power Rangers again

Because it was too hectic.

Tommy woke up and he gave Ann a Power Ranger award.

It had Valour written on it because Ann had helped a Power Ranger.

The End.

After testing out the hero role on me, Natasha invented an alarming monster and then became the hero of her own story and won her own medal.

The description of the monster made us both laugh; earlier terrors about abuse can sometimes be contained through laughter.

The Man Eating Guagwoga

The man eating giant called the Guagwoga only eats people from Panama.

Because they have the hatty taste.

And when he's feeling cold

He goes to the West Indian to have some Hottentots to warm him up.

When he's feeling hot he goes to the North Pole and eats Eskimos to make him feel cold.

Because Eskimos are like ice-cream to him.

After the invention of the Guagwoga Natasha asked me for a gruesome story from the Caribbean. I told her the story of *Big-Gut, Big-Head, Stringy-Leg*:

Big-Gut, Big-Head, Stringy-Leg

There were three boys went out hunting – Big-Gut, Big-Head and Stringy-Leg.

They walked and walked and walked until they came to a huge hole with one banana tree in it, with one big ripe bunch of bananas on it.

They wanted these bananas.

Brother Big-Head said to Brother Big-Gut

'You go up and get it and bring it down and let me eat.'

And Brother Big-Gut said,

'No man you go up my gut is too big.'

So Brother Big-Head said to Brother Stringy-Leg,

'You go up.'

Stringy-Leg said,

'No man I can't go up. My leg is so small it may break.

You go up.'

Big-Head said,

'No. You go, my head is too big. If I go, when I go, My head will burst and I will kill myself.'

So they all teased each other.

Big-Head went up first.

Just as he was going to put his hand on the bananas, his head swung back and he fell down and mashed himself up.

And Brother Big-Gut laughed till his gut burst.

Brother Stringy-Leg ran so (to carry the news) his leg popped.

We thought that was a silly enough story and very like Natasha's own sense of humour. Natasha said she wanted to tell me the second part of her story: *The Death of The Guagwoga*. Natasha's depiction of herself as the Giant Detector was a heroic role for her and one experienced in life as well as her story. She had rooted out the Guagwoga as much as ever you can root out the memory of a man who abuses a two-year-old child. What a giant he must have seemed when she was so small and so afraid. We laughed about the Giant Detector eating earwigs on toast. Natasha has her own greed for tuna sandwiches which she consumes with a secret passion. A connection between past and present.

The Man Eating Guagwoga Meets The Giant Detector

The Giant Detector is a lady and has won lots of awards for detecting giants and rooting them out.

So she is searching for the Guagwoga because she has heard about him and is determined to get him.

So as she is eating her earwigs on toast,

She wonders how to catch him.

She thought of an idea.

She would offer herself as a sacrifice to the Guagwoga.

She put down her toast and went off to find him.

She took a strong chain with her and set off to Giant Country.

Where she was sure the Guagwoga would be.

She found him asleep.

And she woke him up and said:

'You can't catch me'.

The Guagwoga gave a mighty roar.

Floods of people were coming to see what was happening,

And he ran after her.

By this time the Man Eating Giant Detector had taken her chain,

spun it around and tossed it on to the Guagwoga.

She strangled him and put him to death and killed him.

And she got an award for being the bravest lady.

Natasha drew pictures of the Guagwoga and the Man Eating Giant Detector. Later I found a picture she had drawn of herself aged eight, a child with the body of a woman, damaged by sexual abuse, gruesome indeed. We looked at this proud heroic figure of the Giant Detector and compared the two. She was proud of herself and her story. Here is a way to wish for Natasha, a rhyme from Mother Goose to say in hope;

Star light, star bright,

First star I see tonight,

I wish I may, I wish I might,

Have the wish I wish tonight.

Ranjit's Hero: The Asian Footballer

Ranjit is an Asian boy who has been in care since he was three when his mother became psychiatrically ill. He has one sister who is five years older than him. Brother and sister lived together in a children's home for four years, then Ranjit went to a foster family before settling with his present carers where hopefully he will stay until he leaves care. His sister has a small flat and they see each other on a regular basis. He is now twelve.

Ranjit has found it difficult to make attachments to any parenting figures but he is slowly relaxing in his present family where he has lived for a year. His carers are loving and sympathetic to his needs but do not make emotional demands which he cannot meet. However, they expect Ranjit to respect the rules of the family, which he does. He is beginning to learn to trust and has an especially close relationship with his foster father and goes to him for advice and help.

Ranjit is especially loyal to his birth family so it was difficult to explore the trauma of his mother's illness which precipitated his being taken into care. However, he can explore his feelings and fears through storymaking and he has been able to express his sorrow about the loss of his mother. He does remember a great deal about the incident which brought him into care and he made a story about this. Ranjit says he really enjoys our time together and that was a big surprise to him. He thought he would hate it.

I have seen Ranjit for over a year and at the moment his stories are about a hero who wants to be a footballer – the best in the world. We have constant arguments about the merits of Manchester United and Liverpool. I have high status because my father once worked for Manchester United but for Ranjit the Liverpool team are gods.

Liverpool Magic

There are two football players, Stan Collingwood and Steve MacNamara.

They are on holiday, they don't know where.

They got lost and found themselves in a swamp of orange slime with green slime and white slime.

It was radioactive but they thought it was a joke.

Then they found they were lost with no one to help them.

They were scared.

Stan who had just moved to play for Liverpool said:

'Oh, help I just went on holiday and now my career is coming to an end.'

Their feet got stuck and radiated.

They thought their feet looked good being radiated.

Steve said

'This could do something good for us.

Maybe make us better footballers.'

It was going to be good for them

They were afraid of getting cancer later but they would get someone to help them.

Three other players from Liverpool found the two that were lost.

They had followed their footsteps and the football boots.

They kept following till they found them but Stan and Steve were so stuck they couldn't come out.

So the two rescuers got a big stick and dragged them out and they found their way home.

The doctor cured them of the radiation when they got to the UK.

They became the best footballers in the world.

They never told anyone what happened.

They said they had practised really hard to get better.

Which they did.

They didn't want other people to be the best players in the world.

So by keeping their secret they lived happily ever after.

Secrets were a key theme for Ranjit; could he trust his new carers with his feelings about his family. He met his sister often and wanted more contact with his parents but was scared to ask in case he was disappointed. So often at this time there were secret phone calls.

Ranjit also wanted his family to be proud of him so 'good enough' wasn't good enough. You had to be the best. This was his dream and consolation for the loss of his family. Pain and hurt were his parents' experience and treatment with all the high-tech of hospital. Always having to take medicine. Don't tell anyone about the shame of mental illness. Ranjit began to consider the integration of his life and told this story.

The Islands of Past, Present and Future

The Islands of Past, Present and Future

Exist in the sea of magic.

The Past Island was blue, translucent, smooth, sticky, stretchy, cold, broken.

It is the longest island.

The Present Island is blue, mouldy with an eye in the middle.

A good eye, sometimes an evil eye.

The Future Island is green.

The biggest island with a huge football in the middle which is egg shaped.

It is slimy, lumpy and bubbly.

The football is safe from the lumpy edges.

On the Island of the Past lives a cowboy and Frankenstein.

They look after the island.

They help each other.

Sometimes they argue.

They were exploring together because they were friends.

They found the island.

They found another two islands but they left them.

They enjoy living on Past Island.

They curl up in the slime

And bury themselves in it.

On the Present Island lives the Green Power Ranger.

He lives alone.

He misses all his companions.

He was naughty being a Power Ranger.

so they sent him away

and he found this place.

He just looked after it.

Makes sure no one comes

Because he wants it to himself.

The Future Island is inhabited by a dragon.

He shares his space with a turtle and a tiger.

On the back of the dragon is the man that told the dragon to find the island

And he flew around until he found it.

Then he brought his friends.

The man on the dragon's back is a warrior.

One day all the islands come together and make one island.

And in the end they all learn to live together

Not argue so much.

And accept each other.

The Past, Present and Future.

Ranjit sometimes felt lost in the world. He felt bad inside about his mother's illness. He worked hard to develop his running skills and build up his body. It was a dream but he was going to try to be a footballer. I told him the story of *Heron and Humming Bird*.

Heron and Humming Bird

Heron and Humming-Bird lived on the shores of the ocean in the east.

One day Humming-Bird came to Heron and said,

'Let us race.'

Heron answered, 'I can't fly. I can't do anything.'

But Humming-Bird kept teasing him to race and finally Heron gave in.

They agreed to race from the ocean in the east to the ocean in the west. So they placed themselves at the edge of the water and began.

Heron had barely lifted his wings when Humming-Bird was out of sight, and he raised himself slowly flapping at an even pace. When darkness came Humming-Bird went to a tree and stopped there for the night; but Heron kept steadily on, and shortly before daylight he was at the place where Humming-Bird was sitting.

Day came – Heron had travelled a long distance ahead and the sun was well up before Humming-Bird had passed him.

Next night Humming-Bird had to rest again, and again Heron went by him but this time about midnight.

Humming-Bird did not pass him again till noon.

The third night, Heron caught up with Humming-Bird before midnight, and Humming-Bird did not go by him until late evening.

But then he had to stop once more and Heron soon overtook him.

So Heron got to the western ocean far ahead.

It was early morning when he arrived and he began hunting for fish.

Humming-Bird did not arrive till noon.

Then Humming-Bird said to Heron 'I did not believe you could get here first for I can dart all around you and all over you'.

Native American Muskogee

Ranjit drew a picture of his hero. He called him Sunny the Striker and narrated this story.

Sunny the Striker

Sunny the Striker is ace at kicking the ball into the net past the goalkeeper even if it is David James.

Sunny the Striker has clothed himself in Liverpool colours so sunny that nobody can get inside and hurt him.

He also has the sun on top of his head.

It is his way of coping *with the vicissitudes of life.*

> (*My line.*
>
> *I asked to include it because I'd just read it in a book.*
>
> *We both liked it.*)

They are many.

Cousin who is a pain doesn't keep promises

Mum and dad OK for £100 for birthdays

But they are much better in health.

But not enough to be parents.

Sister's doing well

Found a boyfriend who boxes and is very very kind.

So all in all Sunny really feels sunny

So instead of the sun

the colours of Liverpool are protecting Sunny from the world.

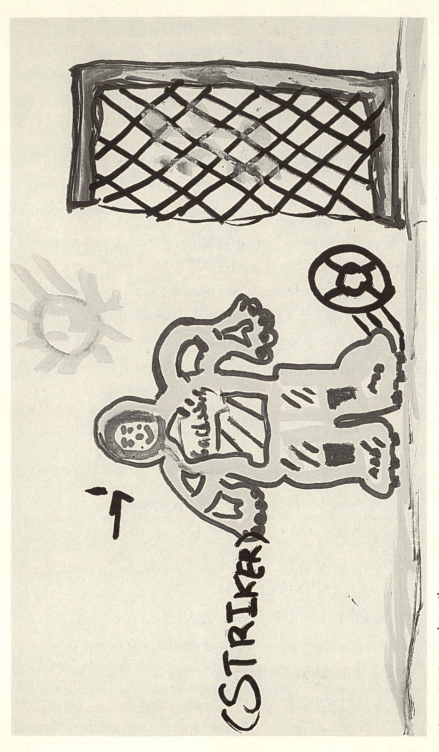

Figure 6.4 Sunny the striker

> Sunny is sunny enough inside to throw a bit of warmth to everyone.
>
> And when he is a world famous footballer adored by the crowds
>
> the first Asian to be a football player,
>
> the sun will shine right out.
>
> And he will feel proud.
>
> His sister will be proud
>
> And his sister's boyfriend
>
> And mum and dad.

We both noted how Sunny was wearing layers and layers of protective clothing as he played and even the goal mouth looked menacing.

Ranjit said that he wanted his family to be proud of him. He carried the scars of their past sadness and felt he must be the one to be the best. His sister told him he must be the best.

We explored this need and that his responsibility was for himself first and foremost. How could he throw off some of that protective clothing when it got too hot to wear? But dreams and hope are necessary and Ranjit is a good footballer. We made a teasing story together about Sunny the greatest footballer in the world.

> Sunny was offered a job as a footballer with Manchester United and he turned it down.
>
> He played for Liverpool the best football club the world.
>
> Ann thinks Sunny has no idea about anything as regards football.

Ranjit told this story with great dramatic effect, pausing after Manchester United to tease me a little more. We thought about the fun of making stories and having hope for an exciting future. We worked out what you have to do to be a footballer. How to get noticed by a club. He already played very well for his school team. Was that enough?

Figure 6.5 A drawing of Ranjit's brain

Ranjit was gaining more confidence and trust towards his foster carers and he was able to talk about seeing his parents. Communication between the two families began so he didn't have to be secretive anymore.

He made a drawing of his brain: footballer self, family, and empty spaces for the future.

Brian's Family Story

Brian told his story when he was knew that he would stay with his present carer long term. He was happy there after frightening years with his mother who had a personality disorder. Brian's story was about being a hero in a family.

Bart Simpson's World

Bart Simpson's world is his house.

He lives there with Lisa and his mum and dad.

Bart is going playing.

He meets a bully boy called Nelson.

Nelson says 'I'm a hero'

Poor old Bart puts his hands over his ears and falls into the sand.

Nelson kicks his head.

The baby comes to the rescue of Bart who changes into Bat man and becomes a hero.

Nelson the bully sticks a pick into his own head by mistake and Bat Man Bart comes to his rescue.

He pulls the pick out of his head and takes Nelson to hospital.

Bart meets a dragon and stops it hurting the family.

He puts a dustbin over its head.

The dragon gets the dustbin off its head

But Bart gets a water hose and put the dragon's fire out.

The End.

Fishy Tales

Pamela's Mermaid

The Walt Disney version of *The Little Mermaid* is commonly reframed by children, most often with the mermaid as victim.

Pamela's story was more heroic, an exploration of a different world where the mermaids had power. A hopeful story told while she was waiting for social workers to find her a permanent family. If only she had a kind father like the one in the story.

Sarah and the Mermaid

There was once a little girl called Sarah who lived by the ocean with her father.

One day Sarah said to her father.

I would like to go out to the ocean to play.

Then the father said yes

So the little girl quickly got changed and went to the ocean and she didn't know she was out too far in the ocean.

The she caught sight of three tails.

They were like mermaids' tails.

Suddenly she saw a mermaid swimming up to her.

And she said 'hello mermaid.'

Then the mermaid said 'hello'.

And the mermaid said 'I'll take you to see the Princess Ariel'

Then the girl said 'I can't swim under water I'll drown'

The mermaid said 'I'll give you a magic potion'.

The mermaid gave her the potion and swam off with her.

When she saw the princess she became friends with her.

The Princess gave her a special present.

Then she had to go because she looked at her waterproof watch

It said 5 pm and she had to be back by then.

She told her father about it all.

Sarah and her father kept the secret of the mermaids and never told anybody else.

I told Pamela an old folk tale about a mermaid.

The Old Man of Cury

One day long ago an old man from Cury was walking on the sands near The Lizard Point in Cornwall when he saw a beautiful girl with fair hair so long that it covered her entire person. She was alone sitting on a rock. On the in-shore side of the rock was a pool of the most transparent water which had been left by the receding tide in the sandy hollow the waters had scooped out. The beautiful girl was arranging her hair in the watery mirror of the pool.

The old man greeted the girl and as soon as she heard his voice she left the rock, sliding right under the water.

The old man thought the girl had drowned. He looked into the pool and saw the girl with her long hair floating and saw that she had a fish's tail.

The old man had heard about mermaids from the fisherman of Gunwalloe and he became frightened. The mermaid was as frightened as he was and tried to hide in the crevices of the rock.

'Don't 'e be afraid, my dear' said the old man 'You needn't mind me. I'm an old man and wouldn't hurt ye any more that your grandfather.'

The mermaid raised her head above the water. She was crying bitterly. She told the old man that her husband and the little ones had been busy at sea all morning and they were all very tired with swimming in the hot sun.

So they went to a cavern in Kynance Cove where her husband slept and the little ones played. While they were all occupied the mermaid thought she would look at the world a little. She could smell the scent of the flowers on the cliffs and she floated on the water from rock to rock looking at the strangeness of the earth until she came to this particular place. She had no idea that the sea was so far out and a long dry bar of sand between her and it.

'What shall I do, oh what shall I do?'

She begged the old man to carry her out to sea. and if he did she would grant him three wishes. The old man agreed and as he carried toward the sea she asked him what he wished for.

'I will not wish for silver and gold but give me the power to do good to my neighbours, first to break the spell of witchcraft, second to charm away diseases and thirdly to discover thieves and recover stole goods.

All this she promised he should possess but he must come to a half-tide rock on another day and she would instruct him how to accomplish the three things he desired.

They had reached the water and taking the comb from her hair she gave it to the old man, telling him he had but to comb the water and call her at any time and she would come to him.

The mermaid loosened her grasp and, sliding off the old man's back into the sea, she waved him a kiss and disappeared.

The old man went to the half-tide rock as agreed and was instructed into many mysteries by the mermaid.

The old man took the mermaid to a secret place where she could see more of the dry land and the strange people who lived on it and had their tails split so they could walk.

When the old man took the mermaid back to the sea she invited him to visit her home where she could make him young if that was his wish. The old man declined.

Two hundred years later the old man's family still have the mermaid's comb.

Some people say the comb is only part of a shark's jaw but those people who do not believe in mermaids are never loveable people.

In both stories the mermaids gave special presents although in Pamela's story the girl goes to the mermaid's country while in the folk tale, the old man refuses the offer.

Pamela thought that moving to different worlds was what had happened to her but in her story the father was waiting for Sarah to take her home. Oh to find such a father; her own was not reliable.

We both liked the idea of combing the water to call up the magic of the mermaids.

Mark's Story: Eric the Scorpion Fish

This is one of Mark's (see Chapter 4) recent stories as he explores his adolescent identity. It seems to integrate aspects of his life in a hopeful way.

The Story of Eric

Eric lived in a river which was full of rubbish.

Eric was a fishlike creature with a long tail, four little fins like legs to help him with swimming and walking.

The water in the river is very cold.

The rubbish is golden.

Everybody throws their rubbish in the river and they don't care about the animals that live in there.

The council are trying to keep the river clean.

But one day they give up so all this rubbish was filling up the river.

And killing the animals.

But only one creature survived and it was Eric.

He was an underwater scorpion fish with a sting in his tail.

He survived in the river because he was born in a pile of rubbish and pollution.

He didn't like it but he was happy that he was still alive.

He didn't want to stay there all his life

Life would be better if he had a clean river.

Two boys came down to the river and saw him.

They put on some gloves, picked him up, and took him to a nice clean river and put him in there.

He lived there and eventually after a long long time in the clean river he met another underwater scorpion fish.

A female fish called Cynthia and they Liked each other.

They had three babies.

One boy two girls, Harry, Laura and Hannah.

They didn't tell the children about the dirty river.

They didn't want them to be brought up in a filthy river.

The End.

On Becoming Somebody Heroic

A delightful new story by Mick Inkpen (1995) called *Nothing* describes a journey to find an identity. The drawings and the story show a small toy abandoned in the attic and forgotten and how he regains his identity.

> 'The little thing in the attic at
> Number 47 had forgotten all about
> daylight. It had been squashed in the
> dark for so long that it could remember
> very little of anything. Stuck beneath
> years of junk, it could not recall how it
> felt to stand up, or to stretch out its arms.
> So long had it been there, even its own
> name was lost.
>
>   'I wonder who I am,'
>
> it thought. But it
> could not remember.

The book explores the journey in words and pictures as Nothing remembers his past and who he is.

> At last Nothing
> remembered who he was.
> Though he had no ears,
> nor whiskers, no tail
> and no stripes, he was
> for certain a little cloth
> tabby cat whose name
> was not Nothing
> but Little Toby
>
> and this, with
> the help of a good wash,
> some scraps of material,

a needle and some
thread is how he
became Little Toby
once more.

CHAPTER 7

Other People's Stories

'Have you any stories like that, guidwife?'

'Ah' she said; 'there were plenty of people that could tell those stories once. I used to hear them telling them over the fire at night; but people is so changed with pride now, that they care for nothing.'

R. Hunt (1916) *Popular Romances of the West of England*

The old woman sighed sympathetically. 'My pretty dear' she said, 'you must be cheerful and stop worrying about dreams. The dreams that come in daylight are not to be trusted, everyone knows that, and even nightdreams go by contraries… Now let me tell you a fairy tale or two to make you feel a little better.'

Apuleius. *The Golden Ass*

The Therapist as Storyteller

As the child and therapist develop their relationship as storyteller and listener and the child's stories are validated by the therapist, the child often asks for a story in return from the therapist. So I often 'tell a tale or two' as we weave our relationship together.

The stories I tell are mostly folk tales, rhymes and riddles, fairy tales. Propp (1968) calls them 'wonder tales', to include both folk and fairy tales. I sometimes imagine myself, as I take the role of storyteller, following the traditions of dear old Mother Goose.

Marina Warner (1994) describes her as a comical witch figure compounded of many fancies and dreams, a fount of female wisdom, an entertainment and butt of the material in which she starred. So in the weaving of the relationship I also help by 'spinning a yarn'.

> There was an old woman tossed up in a basket
> Seventeen times as high as the moon;
> Where she was going I couldn't but ask it,
> For in her hand she carried a broom.
> Old woman, old woman, old woman quoth I,
> Where are ye going to up so high?
> To brush the cobwebs off the sky!
> May I go with you?
> Aye, by-and-by.

Folk Tales

Zipes (1979) defines a folk tale as an oral narrative form used by working people to express the manner in which they perceive nature and their social order and their wish to satisfy their needs and wants.

It is the anonymous working people who have been the carriers and transformers of these tales. Gifted narrators told the tales to audiences who actively participated in their transmission by posing questions, suggesting changes and circulating the tales among themselves. Each community altered and changed the stories as they were handed down over the centuries. It was only in the eighteenth and nineteenth centuries that they were recorded as literary texts.

In his introduction to his collection of Italian folktales Calvino says that these tales in their oft repeated yet constantly varying examination of human vicissitudes, provide a general explanation of life, especially the stage in life which foreshadows the future, birth, departure from home, and through the trials of growing up, the attainment of maturity and the proof on humanity.

In therapy we meet children who have experienced traumas and difficulties which make some of these old tales sound like a description of their actual life experiences. Sometimes the metaphors and images in the stories directly relate to the 'what it felt like' experiences of terror and hurt. But always there is a sense that these are still stories. 'There was there was not. There was a time, and no time', and at the end: 'The tale is over, I cannot lie anymore'.

Each story has many meanings and the one we explore is the one which the child takes as the meaning. The co-constructed relationship between child and therapist is one where the meaning is interleaved between us both and the therapist does not have some kind of godlike knowledge which cannot be accessed by the child.

We all bring our own life experience to the relationship and so in storytelling, as in other aspects of the therapeutic relationship, objective meaning cannot exist. Stories change, we can add characters, throw out others, make out own beginnings and endings because that is the nature of the oral tradition which belongs to the telling of stories.

Marina Warner (1994) points out that the very territory of anonymous storytelling is an area of resistance to tyranny, and also a site of reconciliation and reversal for rejected and ostracised figures. The stories provide a way of putting questions, testing the structure as well as guaranteeing its safety, thinking up alternatives as well as living daily reality but examining that reality.

> 'Storytelling can act to face the objects of derision or fear and sometimes — not always inspire tolerance and even fellow-feeling; it can realign allegiances and remap terrors.'

I have included some stories which have proved helpful and enjoyable for children to whom I have told these tales.

Scary Stories

Sometimes a gruesome story can help us contain our own fears, perhaps make us laugh or be a cathartic experience as we purge our own terrors through a story. However, some children would find them too fearful, so choose carefully.

Keep a Cool Head

Keep a Cool Head is a good winter story. A tall tale which makes us shiver and laugh at the same time. Boys like it because it scares them and girls like it because it serves the boys right.

Keep a Cool Head

He was a graet lad for tellin stories, he had a graet lot o stories, and there was a New Year's Day, ice cam on the loch, you see, an all the young fellows cam there skatin. They were aal oot there wan New Year's Day, ice on the loch, an they were skatin an ther were wan of this boys at geed a bit too far oot, and in the middle o the loch the ice was soft, you ken, an it broake wi him an he geed doon, doon in a hoale, and the other edge o the ice just catched him onder his chin. He slid away under the ice till he came to another hoale, and his head did the same on top o the ice, an when they cam there his heid just stuck on again…the frost was that strong, you ken, till it just froze his heid on again!

In the evenin then they were sittin aroond the haerth tellin stories, and this boy was there too, and he was gotton some of the cowld wi his dip in the cowld watter, you know, and he start to sneeze. An he was gan to blow his nose – they just blow their nose wi their fingers then, you ken – an he was gan to blow his nose, an wi the haet, it was kind of thaaed the ice aboot his neck, you ken; he aimed his heid in the fier!

David Work, from *Scottish Traditional Tales*.

The Flying Head

The *Flying Head* is a very popular monster story where the monster is defeated by a clever, brave woman.

Descriptions of eating and swallowing are constant themes of the play of children who have been hurt. Children who have been sexually abused often say how enormous the adult seems and when they came close and touched them, it was like being swallowed. The vengeance described in this story is an important release. 'Flying Head fled screaming, screaming, screaming...' The repetition is a chorus which the child can shout.

The Flying Head

In days long past evil spirits and monsters preyed upon humans. As long as the sun was shining the monsters hid in deep caves, but on stormy nights they came out of their caves and prowled around the earth.

The most terrible of all was the great Flying Head.

This was a scowling head without body.

Its skin was so thick and matted with hair that no one weapon could penetrate it.

Two huge bird wings grew from either of its cheeks and the Flying Head had a mouth full of huge fangs with which it seized and devoured its prey.

And everything was prey for this monster.

Every living thing.

One dark night a woman with her baby was sitting alone.

Everyone had fled because someone had seen the great Flying Head darting among the treetops in the forest.

The young mother said to herself

'Someone must make a stand against this monster.

It might as well be me'.

So she built a big fire heating in the flames a number of large red-hot glowing stones.

She sat waiting and watching until suddenly the Flying Head appeared in the door.

She pretended not to see it and acted as if she was cooking a meal.

She pretended to eat some of the red-hot rocks.

'What wonderful food,' she said. 'Has anyone feasted on such a meal!'

Hearing this the Monster cold not stop himself.

He opened his jaws wide and seized and swallowed in one mighty gulp, the whole heap of glowing hissing rocks.

As soon as it had swallowed the stones, the monster gave a terrible cry which sounded throughout the land.

Flying Head fled screaming, screaming, screaming over the mountains, streams and forests, screaming so that the biggest trees were shaking, screaming until the earth trembled, scream-ing until the leaves fell from the branches.

At last the screams were fading away in the distance, fading, fading, fading until they were heard no more.

Then the people everywhere could take their hands from their ears and breathe safety.

After that the Flying Head was never seen again, and nobody knows what became of it.

Native American Iroquois.
Adapted from *American Indian Myths and Legends*

Little Red Riding Hood: The Girl and the Wolf

'We keep the wolves outside by living well'

Angela Carter (1979) *The Company of Wolves*

Little Red Riding Hood has many forms and many interpretations. Zipes (1993) points out that it contains elements of a warning tale, an initiation tale, a fairy tale and a fable. It focuses on relations between sex and gender roles and in some versions poses the question of violence and sexism. The story has all the functions of a narrative: the departure from home, meeting the villain, arrival at what seems to be a safe place, the comic interlude with the wolf then the fall of fortune of the protagonist. In some versions there is a happy ending; in others Red Riding Hood does not escape the wolf.

The literary versions of Perrault and Grimm emphasise male rape fantasies of the violence of men against a little girl who in some aspects is seductive and deserves her fate. Classic illustrations of the story from Dore onwards reinforce the rather coquettish girl unafraid of the wolf, but nonetheless victim to the male.

This vulnerability to the violence of the male may need to be expressed by a young child who feels that she has been swallowed by the wolf. The ambiguity of the story and the multiplicity of the themes makes it an interesting story for children in therapy. Some children explore that feeling of being swallowed and eaten by the wolf and being stuck in his stomach. If nobody has helped, then the ending expresses 'what it felt like' being abandoned to a terrible ordeal. Other children explore 'it must be my fault' and how that ideas is present in the story and illustrations.

I have included the Perrault version of 1697 which has grandmother and Little Red Riding Hood eaten by the wolf; no escape or rescue by the woodcutter or father.

The dangers of wolves are expressed in the moral written by Perrault at the end of the tale — a warning that not all wolves are rough creatures but can be smooth and sophisticated in their approaches.

The Little Red Riding Hood

Once upon a time there was a little village girl, the prettiest that had ever been seen.

Her mother doted on her.

Her grandmother was even fonder, and made her a little red hood, which became her so well that everywhere she went by the name of Little Red Riding Hood.

One day her mother, who had just made and baked some cakes, said to her:

'Go and see how you grandmother is, for I have been told that she is ill. Take her a cake and this little pot of butter.'

Little Red Riding Hood set off at once for the house of her grandmother, who lived in another village.

On her way through a wood she met old Father Wolf.

He would have very much liked to eat her, but dared not do so on account of some woodcutters who were in the forest.

He asked her where she was going.

The poor child, not knowing it was dangerous to stop and listen to a Wolf said:

'I am going to see my grandmother, and am taking her a cake and a pot of butter which my mother has sent to her.'

'Does she live far away?' asked the Wolf.

'Oh yes' replied Little Red Riding Hood 'it is yonder by the mill which you can see right below there and it is the first house in the village.'

'Well now' said the Wolf 'I think I shall go and see her too. I will go by this path and you go by that path and we'll see who gets there first.'

The Wolf set off running with all his might by the shorter road and the little girl continued on her way by the longer road.

As she went she amused herself by gathering nuts, running after the butterflies and making nosegays of the wild flowers which she found.

The Wolf was not long in reaching the grandmother's house.

He knocked *Toc Toc*.

'Who is there?'

'It is your little granddaughter Red Riding Hood' said the Wolf disguising his voice.

'And I bring you a cake and a little pot of butter as a present from my mother.'

The worthy grandmother was in bed not being very well and cried out to him:

'Pull out the peg and the latch will fall.'

The Wolf drew out the peg and the door flew open.

Then he sprang upon the poor lady and ate her up in less than no time, for he had been more than three days without food.

After that he shut the door, lying down in the grandmother's bed and waited for Little Red Riding Hood.

Presently she came and knocked *Toc Toc*.

'Who is there?'

Now Little Red Riding Hood on hearing the Wolf's gruff voice was at first frightened but thinking that her grandmother had a bad cold, she replied:

'It is your little granddaughter Red Riding Hood and I bring you a cake and a little pot of butter from my mother.'

Softening his voice the Wolf called out to her:

'Pull out the peg and the latch will fall.'

Little Red Riding Hood pulled out the peg and the door flew open.

When he saw her enter the Wolf hid himself in the bed beneath the counterpane.

'Put the little cake and butter on the bin' he said 'and come up on the bed with me.'

Little Red Riding Hood took off her clothes but when she climbed up on the bed she was astonished to see how her grandmother looked in her night-gown.

'Grandmother dear what big arms you have!'

'The better to embrace you my child.'

'Grandmother dear what big legs you have!'

'The better to run with my child.'

'Grandmother dear what big ears you have!'

'The better to hear with my child.'

'Grandmother dear what big eyes you have!'

'The better to see with my child.'

'Grandmother dear what big teeth you have!'

'The better to eat you with.'

With these words the wicked Wolf leaped upon Little Red Riding Hood and gobbled her up.

Moral

One sees here that young children,
Especially pretty girls,
Polite, well-taught, and pure as pearls,
Should stay on guard against all sorts of men.
For if one fails to stay alert, it won't be strange
To see one eaten by a wolf enraged.
I say a wolf since not all types are wild,
Or can be said to be the same in kind.

Some are winning and have sharp minds.
Some are loud or smooth or mild.
Others appear just kind and unriled.
They follow young ladies wherever they go.
Right into the halls of their very own homes.
Alas for those who've refused the truth:
The sweetest tongue has the sharpest tooth.

From: Perrault's *Fairy Tales*

We use this story critically looking at all the images which reinforce the idea that women are responsible for the violence of men and for their own abuse. It might be of interest for the therapist to know the original version of the story. According to Zipes (1993) it is a seventeenth century tale from the southeast of France and the North of Italy where sewing was an important home industry and women told stories of their sexual and social initiation.

This was a story of working women; the short path of pins and the longer path of needles has implication for women who earned their living by sewing. It was a tale told by adults with a ribald sexuality.

Little Red Riding Hood

Once there was a little girl in a village, and she was called Little Red Riding Hood because of the way she adorned her hair with poppy flowers.

One Saturday afternoon her mother sent Red Riding Hood to her grandmother with a pot of honey and some cakes.

On her way she amused herself by listening to the songs of birds and by gathering nuts and flowers.

But time passed so quickly that it soon became night, and she began to walk faster through the forest.

There she met the Wolf and the Wolf asked her:

'Where are you heading my little girl?'

'I'm taking a pot of honey and some cake to my grand-mother who lives in the first house of the next village,' she answered.

So he asked her;

'What path are you taking?'

'The path of needles to mend my dress which has a hole in it.'

The Wolf left the little girl and took the path of pins which was shorter.

When he arrived at the grandmother's house he tapped at the door

Tick-tock

And the grandmother said;

'Pull the latch, turn the knob and the door will open'

Later when Red Riding Hood arrived he said to her

'Well light the fire.'

'There's some blood on the side of the chimney and I want you to cook it.'

So Red Riding Hood lit the fire and put the pan on top, and poured the blood into it.

While the blood was cooking the pan said to her

'Grubby grub grub

It's grandma's blood.'

Ah the little girl said

'Did you hear Grandma what the pan said?'

'Oh those are just evil spirits in the chimney,' the Wolf responded.

When the blood was cooked Red Riding Hood ate a little of it but she did not like the taste.

Then she went and sat down beside the Wolf believing that he was her grandmother.

'What a large head you have grandma' she said

'That's because of old age my little one.'

'What large legs you have grandma.'

'The better to run, my child.'

'What long hair you have grandma.'

'That's because of old age my child.'

'What big arms you have grandma.'

'The better to catch you with my child.'

'What big teeth you have Grandma'

'The better to eat you with my child.'

But he was still digesting the Grandmother and the little girl knew it was the wolf.

'I want to go pee-pee Grandma,' she said

'Make pee-pee here,' the wolf responded

'Oh but I've also got to make cacka Grandma,'

'Make cacka here,' the wolf responded

'Oh that will smell bad,' the little girl said.

'If you're afraid that I'll escape tie a rope around me and you can hold me.'

So the Wolf attached a rope to her and the little girl went outside where she took a small knife out of her pocket, cut the rope and escaped.

The Wolf ran after her in pursuit but he met up with a hunter who killed him.

Then Red Riding Hood returned home to her mother and told her the story.

Adapted from a version collected by Charles Joisten

There are many other versions of the story including Angela Carter's erotic version *The Company of Wolves* (1979) and the straight vengeance of Thurbur's short version when Red Riding Hood takes out a revolver from her basket and shoots the wolf with the moral that:

'It is not so easy to fool little girls nowadays as it used to be.'

Teeny-Tiny

This is a repetitive story really exploring fear at night and it is fun to use as repetition of the lines acts as a container for fear and the final strategy seems sensible in the circumstances. Very small, young children enjoy this story.

Teeny-Tiny

There was once a teeny-tiny woman who lived in a teeny-tiny house all on her teeny-tiny lone.

One day she went out for a teeny-tiny walk, and came to a teeny-tiny churchyard, where she picked up a teeny-tiny bone.

Then she went back to her teeny-tiny house and had her teeny-tiny tea and went to her teeny-tiny bed.

As she lay in her teeny-tiny bed, she heard a teeny-tiny voice saying,

'Give me my bone.'

The teeny-tiny woman was teeny-tiny frightened, so she pulled her teeny-tiny bedclothes over her teeny-tiny head.

And the teeny-tiny voice said a teeny-tiny louder,

'Give me my bone.'

The teeny tiny woman was a teeny-tiny more frightened and she pulled the bedclothes a teeny-tiny tighter.

Presently the teeny-tiny voice said in a teeny-tiny shriek

'Give me my bone.'

Then the teeny-tiny woman sat up in her teeny-tiny bed, and took the teeny-tiny bone off her teeny tiny window, and said,

'TAKE IT.'

More than One Kind of Mother

The Neglectful Mother

I use this story to describe the some ideas about the meaning of mother, birth mother and the one who nurtures the child.

The Neglectful Mother

Crow had been sitting on the eggs in her nest for many days, and she grew tired of it and flew away.

Hawk came by and found nobody on the nest.

'The person who owns this nest must no longer care for it.

What a shame for those poor little eggs.

I will sit on them and they will be my children'.

She sat for many days on the eggs and finally they began to hatch.

Still no Crow came by.

The little ones all hatched out and Hawk flew about getting food for them.

They grew bigger and bigger, their wings grew strong and finally it was time for mother Hawk to take them from the nest.

After a while, Crow finally remembered her nest.

When she came back she found the eggs hatched and Hawk taking care of her little ones.

'Hawk you must return these little ones' said Crow.

'Why?'

'Because they are mine'.

Hawk said;

'You laid the eggs but you had no pity on the poor things. You left them.

I came and sat on the nest, and hatched them, fed them, and now I lead them about.

They are mine and I won't return them.'

Crow said to the little ones;

'My children, come with me.

I am your mother.'

But the little ones said they did not know her.

'Hawk is our mother' they said.

When Crow couldn't get the children to come with her she said:

'Very well I'll take Hawk to court and we'll see who has the right to these children'.

So Mother Crow took Mother Hawk before the King of the Birds.

Eagle said to the Crow:

'Why did you leave your nest?'

Crow hung her head and had no answer to that.

But she said:

'When I came back to my nest I found my eggs already hatched and Hawk taking care of my little ones.

I have come to ask that Hawk return the children to me'.

Eagle said to Mother Hawk:

'How did you find this nest of eggs?'

Hawk said:

'Many times I went to the nest and found it empty.

I took pity on the eggs and I sat on them and hatched them.

Then I went about getting food for them

I worked hard and brought them up and they have grown'.

Mother Crow said:

'But they're my children. I laid the eggs'.

The King of the Birds said to the Mother Crow:

'If you really had pity on your little ones why did you leave the nest for so many days?

And why are you demanding to have them now?

Mother Hawk is the mother to the little ones,

for she has fasted and hatched them and flown abut searching for their food.

Now they are her children'.

Mother Crow said to the King of the Birds:

'King you should ask the little ones which mother they choose to follow.

They know enough to know which one to take'.

So the King said to the little ones:

'Which mother will you choose?'

Both answered together:

'Mother Hawk is our mother. she's all the mother we know'.

Crow cried: 'No I'm your only mother',

The little Crow children said:

'In the nest you had no pity on us, you left us.

Mother Hawk hatched us and she is our mother'.

So it was finally settled as the little ones had said.

They were the children of Mother Hawk who had pity on them in the nest and brought them up.

Mother Crow began to weep.

The King said to her:

'Don't cry. It's your own fault.

This is the final decision of the King of the Birds'.

So Mother Crow lost her children.

Native American. Cachet.
Adapted from *American Indian Myths and Legends*

Loss of the Family

Why Gypsies are Scattered about the Earth

The first story is a sort of metaphor for neglect or indifference of the importance of the child as a individual. A sense of loss by default.

Why Gypsies are Scattered about the Earth

Once long ago, a gypsy and his family were travelling along in their wagon.

His horse was old and thin and not steady on his legs and as the gypsy's family grew the horse found it harder to pull the wagon so full of children.

As the wagon rolled on getting heavier and heavier as the children jumped about, it began to rock from side to side.

Pots and pans would go flying off the wagon and now and then a child would be thrown to the ground.

It was easy in daylight to go back and pick up the pots and pans and children but you could not see them when it was dark.

And any way there were so many children that nobody kept count.

They were such a tribe.

And the horse plodded on.

The gypsy wagon travelled all over the world and everywhere the wagon went a child went flying off the wagon and was left behind.

More and more and more.

More and more and more and more.

And that is how the gypsies came to be scattered all over the world!

Adapted from *Russian Gypsy Tales*

Johnny Croy and the Mermaid

Johnny Croy is a sad tale about the youngest child being left behind although he was wanted by his mother. The story describes conflict between race and place and different view from members of the family.

Johnny's mother tells her son how to attract the mermaid, although warning him about his endeavours; but when all her grandchildren are to be taken back to Fin-land she keeps the youngest child to live on the land with her.

We sometimes wonder how he will feel when he learns what happened to his parents and brothers and sisters.

Johnny Croy and the Mermaid

One day Johnny Croy went to the shore to look for driftwood.

As he walked along the beach he heard the sound of singing and he saw a mermaid sitting on a rock combing her hair.

Johnny fell in love with her and he crept behind her, sprang
forward and kissed her.

She flung Johnny on the rocks with a blow from her tail and
she slid into the sea leaving her comb behind.

Johnny stood up, shocked, he had never been laid to the
ground like that.

As he stood, he saw the mermaid's comb and he picked it up.

The mermaid saw him pick up her comb.

'Give me back my comb' she cried.

'Not unless you come and live with me' said Johnny.

'I couldn't bear to live on the land' she cried. 'Come with
me and be chief of the Fin-folk.'

Johnny refused and with that the mermaid swam out to sea.

Johnny went home to his mother and told her his story.

'You're very foolish to fall in love with a mermaid but if
you want her you must keep her comb.'

One morning he was awakened by music in his room. He sat
up and saw the mermaid at the bottom of his bed.

'I've come for my comb' she said.

'I'll not give it you' said Johnny 'unless you promise to stay
here and be my wife'.

'I'll make you an offer' said the mermaid. 'I'll live with you
for seven years, if you swear to come with me and all that's
mine, to see my folk at the end of that time.'

Johnny agreed and swore to keep the bargain.

The mermaid was a wonderful wife and in the seven years she
bore Johnny seven children. As the seven years came to an end
the family made ready for a long journey.

Now on the eve of the last day the youngest child was sleeping
at his grandmother's house. Before midnight the grandmother

made a cross of wire, heated it in the fire and laid it on the bare seat of the youngest child.

He screamed like a little demon.

When morning came the family were ready and went down to the boat. But the youngest child was not there.

Johnny Croy's wife ran up to the house to fetch her youngest child but when she tried to lift him from the cradle a dreadful burning went through her arms.

She went back to the boat tears streaming from her eyes.

As the boat sailed away the folk on the shore could hear her lamenting

'Aloor aloor for my bonny child. that I must leave him to live and die upon the dry land.'

Away and away sailed the boat and no one knows where. Johnny Croy and his beautiful young wife and their six children were never seen again.

Adapted from *The Well at the World's End*

Song

Perhaps the child of Johnny Croy and the mermaid might say Keats' poem to his grandmother. Nothing can ever completely take away the pain of loss so that even a new, nurturing home can seem like a prison.

Song

I had a dove and the sweet dove died;
And I had thought it died of grieving;
O, what could it grieve for? its feet were tied
With a silken thread of my own hand's weaving;
Sweet little red feet! why should you die –
Why should you leave me, sweet bird! why?

You liv'd alone in the forest-tree,
Why, pretty thing! would you not live with me?
I kiss'd you oft and gave you white peas;
Why not live sweetly, as in the green trees?

Song John Keats

A Cradle Song

So consolation with a lullaby.

A Cradle Song

Golden slumbers kiss your eyes,
Smiles awake you when you rise.
Sleep pretty wantons, do not cry,
And I will sing a lullaby:
Rock them, rock them, lullaby.
Care is heavy, therefore, sleep you;
You are care, and care must keep you.
Sleep, pretty wantons, do not cry,
And I will sing a lullaby:
Rock them, rock them, lullaby.

Thomas Dekker

Waiting for a Family

The Captive's Oath

This story describes what happens when you have to wait and wait
for something. You begin by feeling grateful but if you want for a
long long time then all you have in your heart is the desire to destroy.
This can be a reminder to social workers, an explanation for adopters
as well as the children. Also a text for family finders.

The Captive's Oath

The Jinni told the fisherman who had let him out of the jar of yellow copper:

I am one of the rebel Jinni and I rose against Solomon, son of David.

I was defeated.

Solomon, son of David, bade me embrace the Faith of God and obey his behests.

I refused.

The king shut me up in this copper jar upon which he set a seal of lead bearing the name of the Most High, and he ordered the submissive Jinni to cast me into the midmost of the ocean.

I said in my heart: 'whoso shall release me, him I shall make rich forever.'

But an entire century passed, and no one set me free.

Then I said in my heart: 'Whoso shall release me, to him shall I reveal all the magic arts of the earth.'

But four hundred years passed and I remained at the bottom of the sea.

Then I said: 'Whoso releases me, Him will I give three wishes.' But nine hundred years passed.

Then I raged and raved and growled and snorted and said to myself,

'Whosoever will set me free, him will I slay.

Soon you came by and set me free.

Tell me how you wish to die.'

From the Third Night of *The Book of*
The Thousand and One Nights

Explanations for Adults

The Way of a Boy

This book is a memoir by Ernest Hillen of his time interned in a Japanese camp in Java, told through the eyes of a child remembered by the man. It is a most moving account. It could help carers to understand the thoughts and feelings behind some kinds of behaviour which are difficult to comprehend.

The first paragraph describes how a child can become indifferent to hurt and pain.

Kampung Makasar

Yet, squatting there over the stinking latrine, I realised that soon after coming to Makasar, I could think about other people dying, anybody really – and that I could finish those thoughts.

I could think it about Corry Vonk and Puk Meijer and the Staals, who had landed in camp after us, and about people living beside and across from us in the barrack. I could see them dead, and it didn't make me sad: dead was dead. The administration office kept the numbers of deaths secret: they didn't want to scare us. People got sick, went to hospital then disappeared out of the gates on stretchers. It was hard to tell how many died because, with new arrivals from other camps, the barracks stayed packed. I also discovered, after a while in Makasar, that I could walk down our barrack, gloomy even in daylight, past women and children with broken teeth and bleeding gums, hair growing in tufts like Willie's, faces and stomachs and legs bloated from hunger edema and beriberi, boils as big as ping-pong balls, and oozing tropical ulcers for which they had no bandages, nor clothes, nor towels to rip into bandages – and not let myself really see them: pain was pain. Just as I could play with other kids, run around, do mischief – but make no friends, on purpose: friends went away. Just as, by then, I could admit to myself that I wasn't especially brave – all I had was my crazy laugh; that I'd never hunted wild boars on the plantation, only pretended to. Just as I could still my mother's voice in my head because I'd learnt that her common sense, be-true-to-yourself dos and don'ts always had their opposites and that the choice was mine – and if I did wrong it wasn't so hard to forgive myself…

Hunger shrunk bodies here, and fear minds, but they also kept you awake, and you had to be awake to stay alive.'

This second paragraph describes the pleasure in making and destroying. In this case small tanks which had been made with loving care by the boys in the camp.

Tjihapit

…I felt a jolt and at once the tank was rolling fast, then faster and faster, little wheels roaring, and I heard myself screaming – the wild feel of it rocketing down! And plunging from the other hill, just as fast, the enemy. My tank obeyed my every tug to the last second – and so did his. And when we ploughed headlong into each other there was a great crunching, cracking and clattering. The tanks fell apart around us drivers and running down the hills came our crews, jumping, yelping, and thumping each other. We'd done it. Never mind the stupid flies, the stink, being hungry or sick all the time, or the Kempetai. We'd done it. Maybe we were just numbers who had only to bow. But we had worked a long time to build a fine tank and then in a split second marvellously smashed that tank to pieces – because we damn well felt like it.'

There is a epilogue to the book which describes the author's journey back to that past so intensely felt as a boy. The final paragraph describes how difficult it is to reframe the past when the original memories are so strong. We must think of this as we work with children who have experienced fear and terror.

> 'I thought of the place we had just left and that I'd travelled so far to visit,…and realised I was already seeing it again, in my mind's eye, as I'd always seen it, and probably always would. Memory is, finally, all we own.'
>
> E. Hillen (1993) *The Way of a Boy. A Memoir of Java*

On Being My Own Person

These poems explore aspects of identity for the child to expand their ideas about themselves.

The Pet Habit

We begin at the place the child inhabits and for many children that means low self-esteem, a sense of physical disgust. This poems makes that sense of disgust into a 'pet' and something humorous.

The Pet Habit

> I'm fed up people telling me
> I've got a nasty habit.
> But I have, it's true, I do.
>
> I keep it in a box full of dirty straw.
> I feed it nose-pickings and belches,
> Bits of spit and bum-scratches.
> It's a nasty little habit.
> When people ask, 'What's in that box?'
> I say, 'It's my pet habit,'
>
> 'Don't you mean pet rabbit?' They ask.
> 'No' I say, and show them.
> 'That's a nasty little habit,' they say.
>
> Brian Patten (1995) *The Utter Nutters*

Sick of Being Pushed Around

Another embodied poem about lack of physical strength but also the sense of doing something about it and laughing at the results. Success guaranteed in the long term.

Sick of Being Pushed Around?

Sick of being
Pushed around,
I sent away
For a course I'd found
In a Batman comic;
Only cost one pound.
It promised to make me
Musclebound.
I must say I quite
Liked the sound
Of a powerful body
That could astound!

They sent part one,
My arms looked great!
Part two is 'Legs'-
I just can't wait

Colin McNaughton (1987) *There's an
Awful lot of Weirdos in our Neighbourhood*

My Best Pal

Maybe a description of self or a friend but showing loyalty as a strategy for a friendship.

My Best Pal

There's a boy in our class
Name of Billy McMillan,
And everyone knows
He's a bit of a villain.

My mum doesn't like him,
No more does my dad,
They say he's a hooligan;
This makes me mad.

Okay, so he's scruffy
And hopeless at school,
But that doesn't mean he's
An absolute fool.

He's brilliant at spitting
And juggling with balls,
And no one can beat him
At peeing up walls.

He's my best mate
And I think he's just fine,
You can choose your friends,
And I will choose mine.

The Doom Merchants

I really like this poem as it explores those gloomy patterns of thinking – in this case put to good commercial use. Now there's a thought for those labelled *Disorganised/disoriented Category D* in Ainsworth's Strange Situation procedure!

The Doom Merchant

Down in the dumps,
At the end of the road to Rack and Ruin
And just beyond hope,

Jerimiah, The Doom Merchant, has opened for business.
(And a sorry business it is too!)

He sits in his shop painting a gloomy picture of a sea of
troubles,
He is wrapped in a wet blanket.
He has cold feet.
Perched on his shoulder is a Nagging Doubt.

He has Fate in store.
He has a shelf of Bad Tidings.
He sells Dashed Hopes and Storm Warnings.
He sells Misfortunes (they come in threes).
He sells Umbrellas (to be put by for a rainy day).
He sells Hats (labelled: On your head be it).
He sells Traps (to keep the wolf from the door).
He sells Life Jackets and Safety Nets (without guarantees).
He sells Handkerchiefs (to wipe away the bitter tears).

On the Doom Merchant's shop window is a permanent sign:
'CLOSING DOWN SALE –
THE END OF THE WORLD IS NIGH.'

Colin McNaughton (1993)
Making Friends with Frankenstein

Short Rhymes

Short rhymes to say to yourself to keep the doom away.

Little Boy

When I was a little boy,
I washed my mammy's dishes;
I put my finger in my eye,
And pulled out golden fishes.

Jumping Joan

Here am I, little
Jumping Joan, When nobody's with me,
I'm always alone. I see the moon
And the moon sees me
God bless the moon
And god bless me.

All's Done

All's done,
All's said.
to-night
In a strange bed
Alone
I lie.
so slight
So hid
As in a chrysalid
A butterfly.

Mally Whuppie

This is an exciting story about Mally who rescues her sisters and gets the good things in life for them and herself.

She has to trick the giant several times, gets his children killed by the giant, and she is less than kind to the giant's wife. Not the perfect hero, but not a victim either, a great survivor.

Mally Whuppie

Once upon a time there was a man and a wife who had too many children, and they could not get meat for them so they took the three youngest and left them in a wood. It began to be dark and the children were hungry. At last they saw a house and they knocked on the door and a woman came to it, who said:

'What do you want?'

'Please let us in and give us something to eat'.

'I can't do that. My man is a giant and he would kill you if he comes home'.

They begged hard.

'Let us in and we will go before he comes back.'

So she took them in and gave them milk and bread.

But suddenly they heard dreadful voice.

'Fee fie fo fum
I smell the blood of some earthly one

Who have you got there wife!'

And she told him of the three children. The giant said nothing but ordered them to stay the night. Now the giant had three girls of his own and they were to sleep in the same bed as the strangers. The youngest of the three strange girls was called Mally Whuppie and she was very very clever.

She noticed that before she went to bed the giant put a straw rope around her neck and her sisters and around his own girls' necks he put gold chains.

When everyone was asleep Mally changes the chains around and places the gold chains on her sisters' necks and the straw ropes round the giant's children.

In the middle of the night the giant took his club and came into the bedroom and in the dark he hit his own daughters thinking they were the strangers. The giant lay down again thinking he had done a fine job.

Mally Whuppie thought it was time she and her sisters were off so she woke them, told them to be quiet and get out of the house. They ran and ran and never stopped till morning when they saw a grand house in front of them.

It was the king's house and Mally told her story to the king.

He said:

> 'Well Mally you are a very clever girl but if you would go
> back and steal the sword that hangs behind the giant's bed
> then I would give your eldest sister my eldest son to marry'.

Mally said she would try.

So she went back to the giant's house and crept in below his
bed. The giant came home, ate his meal and went to bed.

When Mally heard him snoring she reached over the bed and
grabbed the sword. But as she took it, the bed made a rattle,
and the giant jumped up. Mally jumped out of the door and
ran and ran and he ran and ran until they came to the 'Bridge
of One Hair' and she got over but he couldn't and he says;

> 'Wae worth ye Mally Whuppie never ye come again'.

And she says. 'Twice yet carle I'll come to Spain'.

So Mally took the sword to the king and her sister was married
to his eldest son.

The king said 'You have managed well Mally but if you steal
the purse that lies below the giant's pillow I would marry your
second sister to my second son'.

So Mally set off for the giant' house and hid below his bed
and waited till the giant was snoring.

She slipped her hand beneath his pillow but as she was going
out the giant wakened and she ran and he ran till they came
to the 'Bridge of One Hair' and she got over but he couldn't
and he said;

> 'Woe with ye Mally Whuppie lat ye never come again'

> 'Once yet carle' said she 'I'll come to Spain.

So Mally took the purse to the king and her second sister was
married to the king's second son.

And the king says to Mally:

'Mally you are a clever girl but if you would do better yet and steal the giant's ring that he wears on his finger I will give you my youngest son for yourself.'

Mally goes back to the giant's house and lies herself below the bed until she heard the giant snoring. Mally reached over the bed, got hold of the giant's hand, and pulled and pulled until she got the ring. But just as she got the ring the giant got up and gripped her by the hand and said;

'Now I have caught you Mally Whuppie and if I done as much ill to you as ye have done to me, what would ye do to me?'

Mally said:

'I would put you inside a sack and I'd put the cat and dog inside wi you and a needle and thread and shears and I'd hang you up upon the wall, find a stout stick, take the sack from the wall and bang it with the stick'.

'Well Mally' says the giant, 'I'll do just that'.

So the giant did just that and as Mally is in the sack and the giant goes out looking for the stick, Mally sings out:

'Oh if ye saw what I see.'

'Oh' said the giant' wife,. 'what do ye see Mally?'

But Mally never said a word but 'Oh if you could see what I see'.

The giant's wife begged Mally to take her up in the sack so Mally took the shears and cut a hole in the sack and took out the needle and thread with her and jumped down and helped the giant's wife up into the sack and then she sewed up the hole.

The giant's' wife saw nothing and began to ask to get down again.

But Mally never minded and hid herself at the back of the door.

The giant came back with his stick, took down the sack and began to batter it.

His wife cried 'It's me man' but the dog barked and the cat mewed and he did not know his wife's voice.

Mally came out from the back of the door and the giant saw her and he ran after her. He ran and she ran till they came to the 'Bridge of One Hair' and she got over but he couldn't and he said

'Woe worth you Mally Whuppie. Never you come again'.

'Never more, carle', quoth she "will I come again to Spain.'

So Mally took the ring to the king and she was married to his youngest son and she never saw the giant again.

Adapted from Joseph Jacobs (1892)

How Tenali Rama became a Jester

This is another clever hero, not afraid of anyone, even laughing at the goddess who was made furious by his rudeness but lost her anger when she realised his cleverness.

How Tenali Rama Became A Jester

In a South India village called Tenli there lived a clever Brahmin boy. His name was Rama.

Once a wandering *sanjassi* was impressed with the boy's looks and clever ways. So he taught him a chant and told him:

'If you go to the goddess Kali's temple one night and recite these words three million time, she will appear before you with all her thousand faces and give you what you ask for – if you don't scare her.'

Rama waited for the auspicious day, went to the Kali temple outside his village, and did as he was told.

As he finished his three millionth chant the goddess did appear before him with her thousand faces and two hands.

When the boy looked at her horrific appearance he wasn't frightened.

He fell into a fit of laughter.

The fearsome goddess was offended.

No one had ever laughed at her before.

> 'You little scallywag why are you laughing at me?'

> 'Oh mother we mortals have enough trouble wiping our noses when we catch a cold though we have two hands and only one nose. If you with your thousand faces should catch a cold how would you manage with just two hands for all those thousand runny noses.'

The goddess was furious. She said, 'Because you laughed at me you'll make a living only by laughter. You'll be a *vikatakavi*, a jester.

> 'Oh a *vi-ka-ta-ka-vi*. That's terrific. It's a palindrome. It reads the same from right to left and from left to right.' replied Rama.

The goddess was pleased by Rama's cleverness that saw a joke even in a curse.

She at once relented.

> 'You'll be a *vikatakavi* but you will be jester to a king.'

And she vanished.

Folktales from India

Songs and Stories for the Therapist

Nero and Bertha

This story is about being rewarded for a skill – becoming a rich lady, a nice dream at the end of a hard day. But like all good stories it has many layers of meaning and riches have their price. The reward is given by a bad emperor and Bertha's spinning is lost for ever.

Nero and Bertha

This particular Bertha was a poor woman who did nothing but spin, being such a skilful spinner. One day as she was going along she met Nero, the Roman emperor, to whom she said,

> 'May God grant you good health so good you'll live a thousand years!'

Nero, whom not a soul could abide because he was so mean, was astounded to hear someone wishing him well and he said, 'Why do you say that to me my good woman?'

> 'Because a bad one is always followed by one still worse.'

Nero then said,

> 'Very well bring to my palace all you spin between now and tomorrow morning.'

At that he left her.

As she spun Bertha said to herself,

> 'What will he do with the thread I'm spinning? I wouldn't put it past him to hang me with it. That monster is capable of anything.'

Next morning right on time she went to Nero's palace.

He invited her in, received the thread she had spun and said: 'Tie the end of the ball to the palace door and walk away as far as you can go with the thread.'

Then he called his chief steward and said;

'For the length of the thread the land on both sides of the road belongs to this woman.'

Bertha thanked him and walked away very happy.

She no longer needed to spin for she had become a lady.

When word of the event got around Rome, all the poor women went to Nero in the hope of present such as he had given Bertha.

Bur Nero replied:

'The good old times when Bertha spun are no more.'

Adapted from Calvino (1982) *Italian Folk Tales*

A Work for Poets

I think this poem expresses each person's desire to have made some meaning for their life lived which can be recognised by others.

A Work for Poets

To have carved on the days of our vanity
A sun
A ship
A star
A cornstalk

Also a few marks
From an ancient forgotten time
A child may read

That not far from the stone
A well
Might open for wayfarers

Here is a work for poets —
Carve the runes
Then be content with silence

George Mackay Brown *Following A Lark*

From the Temple Walls of Medinet Habu, Thebes

A place to imagine is important for the therapist confronted with the cruelties of the world. I still imagine the heat and timelessness of Luxor in Egypt, which is also Thebes, and as I get older I cross the Nile in my mind's eye to the Valley of the Kings and remember the monuments of Medinet Habu in the Theban Hills. Medinet Habu is a mortuary temple;

> 'the Mansion of Millions of Years of King Ramessess 111,
> 'United with Eternity in the Estate of Amon.'

It is a place apart, and through its long history, the uses and functions of the building and surroundings have changed. It has been and is a temple, palace, Coptic town, uninhabited ghost town, and now the first or last short stop on the tourists' itinerary in the Valley of the Kings.

It is said that women still bathe in the sacred lake by the temple in the hope of conceiving children. The pool is now so neglected that to survive a bathe would seem more a miracle. But the place has the magic of many lives lived in many ways. The wall paintings and reliefs have images of war, the conquerors and the vanquished, life lived through work and feast and festival, holy images of gods who were masters of the four corners of the universe. The stuff of life and the desire for immortality. It is a world. It changes and is reborn.

I like to remember the heat and the breeze blowing across those Theban hills, the vastness and the isolation of the place. This verse from the *Egyptian Book of the Dead* is written on the north wall of the Osiris Temple and although it is a wish for the joys of Eternity, to me it defines that intense feeling of being alive in the present moment, in a particular place and time.

> 'I recognise I am among the lakes in the
> Field of Offering.
> Here I am strong, I am full of glory
> Here I exist.

I plough the fields. I reap the fields
I am fruitful.
Here I remember.
I do not forget.
I am alive.'

References

Agard, J. (1985) 'Don't call alligator long-mouth till you cross the river.' In *Say It Again, Granny*. London: The Bodley Head.

Ainsworth, M.D.S., Blehar, M.C., Waters, E. and Wall, S. (1978) *Patterns of Attachment*. Hillsdale N.J: Lawrence Erlbaum.

Angelou, M. (1986) *And Still I Rise*. London: Virago Press Ltd.

Bateson, G. (1995) 'A theory of play and fantasy.' *Psychiatric Research Reports 2*, 39–51.

Bateson, G. (1972) *Steps to an Ecology of Mind*. New York: Chandler.

Baudrillard, J. (1990) *Cool Memories*. Trans. Turner, C. London: Verso.

Baudrillard, J. (1993) *The Transparency of Evil*. Trans. Benedict J. London: Verso.

Bloch, E. (1930) 'The fairy tale moves on its own in time.' Quoted in J. Zipes (1979, 1992) *Breaking the Magic Spell*. New York: Routledge.

Bowlby, J. (1969) *Attachment and Loss, Vol. 1. Attachment*. London: Hogarth Press.

Bowlby, J. (1973) *Attachment and Loss Vol. 2. Separation, Anxiety and Anger*. London: Hogarth Press.

Boyden, J. (1990) 'Childhood and policy Makers: a comparative perspective on the globalization of childhood.' In *Constructing and Reconstructing Childhood*. Basingstoke: The Falmer Press.

Bronfenbrenner, U. (1979) *The Ecology of Human Development*. Cambridge, Mass. Harvard University Press.

Bruford, A. and Macdonald, D.A. (1994) *Scottish Traditional Tales*. Edinburgh: Polygon.

Bruner, J. (1986) *Actual Minds, Possible Worlds*. Cambridge. Mass: Harvard University Press.

Bruner, J. (1990) *Acts of Meaning*. Cambridge, Mass: Harvard University Press.

Calvino, I. (1982) *Italian Folktales*. Tr. Martin, G. London: Penguin Books Ltd.

Carter, A. (1979) 'The company of wolves.' In *The Bloody Chamber*. New York: Harper & Row.

Carter, A. (1990) (ed) *The Virago Book of Fairy Tales*. London: Virago Press Ltd.

Cattanach, A. (1992) *Play Therapy With Abused Children*. London: Jessica Kingsley Publishers.

Clarke-Stewart, K.A. (1988) 'The "effects" of infant day care reconsidered; risks for parents, children and researchers.' *Early Childhood Research Quarterly 3*, 293–318.

Cummings, e.e. 'maggie and milly and molly and may.' In *Complete Poems 1904–1962*. New York: W.W. Norton. & Co Ltd.

Donovan, J. (1996) 'Group narrative function in brief dramatherapy.' In A. Gersie (ed) *Dramatic Approaches to Brief Therapy*. London: Jessica Kingsley Publishers.

Dove, R. (1995) *Mother Love*. New York: W.W. Norton & Co. Ltd.

Doyle, R. (1993) *Paddy Clarke Ha Ha Ha*. London: Secker & Warburg Ltd.

Druts, Y. and Gessler, A. (1986) *Russian Gypsy Tales*. Tr. Riordan, J. Edinburgh: Canongate Press.

Dunn, J. (1987) 'Understanding feelings: the early stages.' In J. Bruner and H. Haste (eds) *Making Sense*. London: Methuen & Co. Ltd.

Dunn, J. (1993) *Young Children's Close Relationships*. London: Sage.

Eco, U. (1995) *The Island of the Day Before*. London: Secker & Warburg.

Engel, S. (1995) *The Stories Children Tell*. New York: W.H. Freeman & Company.

Erdoes R. and Ortiz, A. (1984) *American Indian Myths and Legends*. New York: Pantheon Books.

Gergen, K. (1991) *The Saturated Self*. New York: Basic Books.

Gergen, K. (1994) 2nd. edition. *Toward Transformation in Social Knowledge*. London: Sage.

Giraudy, D. (1988) *Picasso The Minotaur*. New York: Harry N. Abrams Inc.

Harris, P.L. (1994) 'The child's understanding of emotion: developmental change and the family environment.' In *Journal of Child Psychology and Psychiatry 35*, 1, 3–28.

Heaney, S. (1990) *New Selected Poems 1966–1987*. London: Faber & Faber Ltd.

Hendrick, H. (1990) 'Constructions and reconstructions of British childhood.' In A. James and B. Prout (eds) *Constructing and Reconstructing Childhood*. Basingstoke: The Falmer Press.

Hillen, E. (1993) *The Way of a Boy*. London: Penguin Books Ltd.

Hunt, R. (1916) *Popular Romances of the West of England*. London: Chatto and Windus

Inkpen, M. (1995) *Nothing*. London: Hodder Children's Books.

Jacobs, J. (1892) *Celtic Fairy Tales*. London: David Nutt.

Jenks, C. (1996) *Childhood*. London: Routledge.

Keizer, B. (1996) *Dancing With Mister D*. London: Doubleday, Transworld Publishers Ltd.

Kitzinger, J. (1990) 'Who are you kidding? Children power and the struggle against sexual abuse.' In A. James and B. Prout (eds) *Constructing and Reconstructing Childhood*. Basingstoke: The Falmer Press.

Laing, R.D. (1995) 'Why did the peacock scream?' In M. Rosen (ed) *A World of Poetry*. London: Kingfisher.

Mackay Brown, G. (1996) *Following a Lark*. London: John Murray Publishers Ltd.

Main, M. (1994) *A Move to the Level of Representation in the Study of Attachment Organisation: Implications for Psychoanalysis*. Annual Research Lecture to the British Psycho-Analytic Society. London, July 6 1994.

Main, M. and Hesse, E. (1990) 'Parents unresolved traumatic experiences are related to infant disorganised attachment status: Is frightened and/or frightening parental behaviour the linking mechanism?' In M.T. Greenberg, D. Cichetti and E.M. Cummings (eds) *Attachment in the Pre-school Years: Theory, Research and Intervention*. Chicago: Chicago University Press.

Main, M. and Solomon, J. (1990) 'Procedures for identifying infants as disorganised/disoriented attachment pattern.' In T.B. Brazelton and M. Yogman (eds) *Affective Development in Infancy*. Norwood: Ablex.

Main, M. and Solomon, J. (1992) 'Disorganised/disoriented infant behaviour in the Strange situation, lapses in the monitoring of reasoning and discourse during the parents Adult Attachment interview, and dissociative states.' In M. Ammaniti and D. Stern (eds) *Attachment and Psychoanalysis*. Rome: Guis, Laterza and Figli.

Main, M. and Weston, D (1981) 'The quality of the toddlers relationship to mother and to father: Related to conflict behaviour and the readiness to establish new relationships.' *Child Development 52*, 932–940.

Markus, H. and Nurius, P. (1986) 'Possible selves.' *American Psychologist 41*, 954–969.

Mayle, P. (1978) (1993) *Where Did I Come From?* London: Pan Books Ltd.

McNaughton, C. (1987) *There's an Awful lot of Weirdos in Our Neighbourhood*. London: Walker Books.

McNaughton, C. (1993) *Making Friends With Frankenstein*. London: Walker Books.

Mead, G.H. (1934) *Mind, Self and Society*. Chicago: University of Chicago Press.

Montgomerie, N & W. (1993) *The Well at the World's End*. Edinburgh: Canongate Press.

Namjoshi, S. (1994) *Feminist Fables*. London: Virago Press.

Namjoshi, S. (1994) *Saint Suniti and the Dragon*. London: Virago Press.

Neisser, U. (1988) 'Five kinds of self-knowledge.' *Philosophical Psychology 1*. New York: Routledge.

Nicholson, B. (1968) *Exhibition April – 15 June 1968*. Basel: Galerie Beyeler.

Patten, B. (1995) *The Utter Nutters*. London: Puffin Books.

Perrault, C. (1969) *Perrault's Fairy Tales*. New York: Dover Publications Inc.

Phillips, T. (1980) *A Humument*. London: Thames & Hudson.

Propp, V. (1968) *Morphology of the Folktale*. rev. edn. Wagner, L and Dundes, A. Austin: University of Texas Press.

Prout, A. and James, A. (1990) 'A new paradigm for the sociology of childhood.' In A. James and A. Prout (eds) *Constructing and Reconstructing Childhood*. Basingstoke: The Falmer Press.

Ramanujan, A.K. (1991) *Folktales From India.* New York: Pantheon Books.

Ricoeur, P. (1981) 'The narrative function.' In J.B. Thompson (ed) *Hermeneutics and the Human Sciences.* Cambridge: Cambridge University Press.

Rosaldo, M. (1984) 'Towards an anthropology of self and feeling.' In R. Schroeder and R. Le Vine (eds) *Culture Theory: Essays on Mind, Self and Emotion.* Cambridge: Cambridge University Press.

Russell, J. (1923) 'John Russell's book of nurture.' In I. Gollancz (ed) *The Babees Book.* London: Chatto & Windus.

Sendak, M. (1993) *We are All in the Dumps with Jack and Guy.* New York: Harper Collins.

Shotter, J. (!989) 'Social accountability and the social construction of "You".' In J. Shotter and K. Gergen (ed) *Texts of Identity.* London: Sage.

Stevenson, R.J. (1860) 'A treasure island.' In S. Miles (ed) (1923) *Childhood in Verse and Prose.* Oxford: Oxford University Press.

Teneze. M.L. (ed) (1970) *Approches de nos traditions orales.* Paris: Maisonneuve et Larose.

Thurbur, J. (1939) 'The girl and the wolf.' In *Fables for our Time and Famous Poems.* New York: Harper.

Tizard, B. (1977) *Adoption: A Second Chance.* London: Open Books.

Tolkien, J.R.R. (1979, 1992) 'On fairy stories.' In J. Zipes *Breaking the Magic Spell.* New York: Routledge.

Turner, V. (1982) *From Ritual to Theater.* New York: New York Performing Arts Publications.

Umphelby, F. (1828) *The Child's Guide to Knowledge.* Simpkin Marshall and Co.

Vygotsky, L. (1978) *Mind in Society. The Development of Higher Psychological Processes.* Cambridge, Mass: Harvard University Press.

Warner, M. (1994) *From the Beast to the Blonde.* London: Chatto & Windus.

Wells, H.G. (1913) reprint (1966) *Floor Games.* London: Quantum Reprints.

White, M. and Epston, D. (1989) *Literate Means to Therapeutic Ends.* Adelaide: Dulwich Centre Publications. republished (1990) as *Narrative Means to Therapeutic Ends.* New York: W.W. Norton.

Wilson, G. (1994) *Prowlpuss.* London: Walker Books.

Zipes, J. (1979) *Breaking the Magic Spell.* New York: Routledge.

Zipes, J. (ed) (1993) *The Trials and Tribulations of Little Red Riding Hood.*

Subject Index

attachment theory 116–19

'bad' child image 62–3
Bad Men 92
Bad-Tempered Dinosaur 107
'Banana Man' story 102–3
Barry, 'beginning story' example 77–8
Bart Simpson in the Forest 158–9
Bart Simpson's World 187–8
Battle of the Birds 78–9
'believable' stories 3
Big Bang 109–10
Big-Gut, Big-Head, Stringy-Leg 175
Biggest Monster in the World 68
Bird Woman 74
Black and White Families 172
black identity stories 86–96, 168–73
body awareness 41
Book of Nurture 43–4
Book of the Thousand and One Nights 217
Brian, fear stories 79–86, 187–8
Bungalow 127–9

Captive's Oath 216–17
'car land' story 87–8
care system, children in 156–64

abandonment stories *see* loss and abandonment stories
Abigail, loss stories 135-41, 147-8
adolescent stories *see* Mark
adopted children 120-1
case examples 122-56
Adventures of Good Man 111
African Family 172–3
alienated meaning 76
All's Done 224
alternative stories 18
American Indian Myths and Legends 200, 212
Andrew, loss stories 148–56, *149*
angels, children as 63
Angus, loss stories *157*, 158–62, *159*
'apple crumble' story 11–12
'Arnold Schwarzenegger' story 77

carers
attitudes of 31–2
explanations for 218–20
relationship with child 117–19
Carol, foster child example 162
'Change Three Things' Game 42
child development theory 7
child-therapist relationship *see* therapist–child relationship
childhood defined 61–6
British social construction 61–5
new paradigm 65–6
Chimney Sweep 63–4
communication, importance of 12–13
Company of Wolves 208
confidentiality 67–8
containers, stories as 3, 77, 84
contextual variants, attachment theory 117
cooling function of stories 77
Cosworth Family 48–9
Cradle Song 216
Crash 126
'crazy family' picture 159

Crazy Power Ranger 173–4
creative play 40–9
Crocodile 54
'Crow and Her Children' 2–3
cruelty and love, separating 59–60
cultural influences 15, 25
ecological systems 34
cultural myths, 4–5

Dark Cave 104
'dark, dark wood' story 105
David, monster crocodile story 72
developmental play paradigm 40
dialogues, internalising 14
'dinosaur' story 85
disaster themes 122–7
Disgusting Monster 136
'disorganised/disoriented' category 118–19
divergent narratives 5
dominant stories 18
Don't Call Alligator Long-Mouth Till You Cross River 114
Doom Merchants 222–3
Dragon Country 90–2
Dragon Family 98–9
Dream of Chuang Tzu 166
dream stories *see* hero stories

drug addicted parents, loss stories 148–56
'dyad' unit of analysis 35–6

ecological research 35–6
ecological systems 33–6
ecological transitions 35
Egyptian Book of the Dead 232
Elmore, knife story 6–7
embodied play 40–4
emotions
child's understanding 119–20
social construction of 15–17
Evil World 151–2
exceptional-ordinary links 24–9
exosystem structure 34
'explanations for adults' stories 218–20
'extended self' concept 30

Fairy Tales 205
fairy tales 25, 166–7, 195–6
Falsehood Corrected 62–3
Family 140

family dolls 48–9, 127–9
'family' story examples 48–9, 127–9, 172–3
fear and loathing stories 2, 75–114
case studies 78–108
exploring meaning 76–8
parents' mental illness 108–14
feeling states 15–17
Female Rip-Tail Roarer 95–6
Fighting Mum and Dad 25–6
Feminist Fables 54, 74
Fizzy, Fizzy Monster 80–1
Floor Games 39
Flying Head 199–200
folk tales 166–7, 195, 196–7
Folktales from India 229
Following A Lark 231
football hero stories 177–85, *184*
Forest (1) 146
Forest (2) 158–9, 160
fostered children 121
framing of play 39–40
Fred 129
From a Humument 69

'gak' 43, 44
'Gaudi', monster story 45–6

'Giant Detector' stories 168, *171*, 176–7
Girl and the Wolf 201–8
Golden Ass 195
Golden River 97–8
Good Boy 63
'good' child image 64
'Guagwoga' stories *170, 171,* 174, 176–7

Hansel and Gretel 8–9
Haunted House (Abigail) 138–9
Haunted House (Rachel) 134–5
heroic stories 165–94
    consolation of stories 166–7
    examples 168–94, *169–71, 184, 186*
    hopeful stories 166
    role of heroes 167–8
Heron and Humming Bird 182–3
hiding themes 88–9
Hop-O'-My-Thumb 9, 14–15
hopefulness in stories 166–7
House of Horrors 111–12
How Tenali Rama Became a Jester 228–9
human figure toys 46–8

'I'-'You' relationship 13
    see also self
identity, stories of 31
initial play therapy meetings 36–7
'innocence' concepts 60
'insecurely attached avoident' category 118
'insecurely attached resistant' category 118
Island of the Day Before 1
Islands of Past, Present and Future 180–1
Italian Folk Tales 231

'Jack and Guy' rhyme 146–7
Jane, nobody story 55–6
Janet, adopted child example 121
Jim, star creature story 52–4
John, monster story 45–6
Johnny, parents story 9–10
Johnny Croy and the Mermaid 213–15
'Johnny on the Railroad' rhyme 146
Joshua, mentally ill parent example 109–10
Jumping Joan 224

Kampung Makasar 218–19
Katherine, fear stories 96–9
Keep a Cool Head 198

language as mediator 8, 14, 18
Lazy Jack 19–21
Lewis, mentally ill parent example 110–14
Little Boy 223
Little Red Riding Hood 201–8
Little Town 145–6
Liverpool Magic 178–9
loathing stories *see* fear and loathing stories
loss and abandonment stories 115–64, 212–16
    adopted children 120–1
    examples 122–56, *123–5, 143, 144, 149, 157, 159*
    attachment theory 116–19
    children in care examples 156–63, *157, 159*
    child's understanding 119–20
    sad songs and gay 163–4

'lost' child image 63–4
Lost Scary Monster 155
'lost' themes 102
love and cruelty, separating 59–60

macrosystem structure 34
maggie and milly and molly and may 148
'magic' themes 97–8
Making Friends with Frankenstein 223
Mally Whuppie 224–8
Man-eating Guagwoga 170, 171, 174, 176–7
Mandy 13–14, 70
    fear and loathing stories 86–96
Margaret, loss stories 142–8, 143, 144
Mark 72–3, 191–2
    fear stories 99–108
Mary, mentally ill parent example 108–9
Mary and Jane, 'control' story 11–13
Mask 153–4
materials for storymaking 39, 40–9
meaning
    exploring through play 24, 76–8
    negotiating 4, 7, 25, 119–20

Meat of the Tongue 16–17
Medinet Habu, Thebes 232–3
meetings, initial play therapy 36–7
mentally ill parents, examples of children with 108–14, 177–86
mermaid stories 47, 88–9, 139–40, 142, 188–91, 213–15
Mermaid World 142
Mermaids 88–9
mesosystem structure 34
microsystem structure 33
Mirror 50–1
'mode of thought' 5–7
Monster Caught 71
Monster Story Again 22–4
monsters
    children as 62–3
    examples of stories 2, 4, 22–4, 45–6, 80–2, 87–8, 90, 136, 155
    love and cruelty 59–60
    messing with 68–73
monstrous others, chasing 69–73
Morphology of the Folktale 167

'Mother Goose' image 196
Mother Love 115
'mother' story 209–12
Mr Nobody 55
Mr Slimy 70
Mrs Disgusting Idiot 150
My Best Pal 221–2
'myself' narrative 130–2
mythical creature toys 46–7
myths 4–5

Narrative Means to Therapeutic Ends 19
narrative mode 5, 7
narrative therapy 17–19
narratives, stories compared 29–31
narrator–listener relationship 3
Natasha, heroic stories 168–77, 169–71
Neglectful Mother 209–12
negotiating meaning 4, 7, 25, 119–20
Nerd's Story 103–4
nero and Bertha 230–1
No Name 94–5
'no talking' sessions 92–3
No Voice 95
'not-play' space 37–8
Nothing 193–4

Oddie Family 141
Old Man of Cury
    189–91
Old Man on the Gump
    160–2
Old Village 100–1
'other', differentiating
    from 'self' 51–9
other people's stories
    195–233
    'being my own
        person' stories
        220–9
    explanations for
        adults 218–20
    folk tales 196–7
    for therapists 230–3
    'loss of family'
        stories 212–16
    'mother' story
        209–12
    scary stories
        198–209
    therapist as
        storyteller 195–6
    'waiting for a
        family' stories
        216–17
'ours' relationship 13
'own identity' stories
    220–9

*Paddy Clarke Ha Ha
    Ha* 38, 40–1, 75,
    115
Pamela, heroic stories
    188–91
paradigmitic mode 5,
    7
parents stories 8–10

'part for whole
    coding' 17
partnership
    agreements,
    child–therapist 8
peek-a-boo game
    55–6
perpetrator–child
    relationship,
    therapist–child
    compared 66–8
Pet Habit 220
pictures, stories from
    123–5, 130–5
*Play Therapy with
    Abused Children* 37
playfulness 3, 4–5
playground rhymes
    64–5
playing methods
    37–8
*Popular Romances of the
    West of England*
    195
Possible Selves 5–6
'Power Ranger'
    stories 47, 96–7,
    156, 139–40,
    173–4
Power Rangers World
    156
pretend play 16, 19
projective play 44–9
Prowlpuss 53–4
psychological reality 7
Purple Slime Monster 90
purpose of stories
    1–21
    developing self
        13–15

finding useful
    stories 17–19
play therapy as
    social
    construction
    8–13
playfulness 4–5
restorying 19–21
social construction
    of emotions
    15–17
therapeutic
    relationship 3
two modes of
    thought 5–7

*Race of the Power
    Rangers* 96–7
Rachel, loss stories
    122–35, *123–5*,
    147–8
'rainbow' story 93
Ranjit, heroic stories
    177–87, *184, 186*
Ravi, monster story
    70–1
reality–fantasy issues
    40
Reeva, monster
    stories 22–4, 30
restorying 19–21
'restraints' 17
rhymes 64, 223–4
River Thames 106
Robber 137
role exploration 57–8
rules of play, case
    examples 79–80,
    135–6, 137
Russian Gypsy Tales
    213

Sad Country 154–5
Sad Songs and Gay 163–4
safety themes 87–9, 93–4, 110–14
Saint Suniti and The Dragon 53, 59
Sally, monster stories 2–3, 4, 5
Sarah 137
Sarah and the Mermaids 188
Scary Dream 138
scary stories 198–209
Scottish Traditional Tales 198
secrets 67–8
secure attachment category 118
'seekers' 167
Self
   differentiating 13–15, 50–74
   childhood defined 61–6
   from 'other' 51–9, 69–73
   love and cruelty 59–60
   extended 30–1
   Possible Selves 5–6
sensory exploration 41–2
separation stories *see* loss and abandonment stories
settings for play therapy 36–40
   framing 39–40

initial meetings 36–7
playing 37–9
sexual abuse 76, 77
   case examples 79–86, 99–108
Sick of being Pushed Around? 221
silence, coping with 86, 92
Silly Story 105
slime 43, 44
Slime Fuck 84–5
Snake and Crocodile 90
Snowstorm 113–14
social construction
   of British childhood 61
   of emotions 15–17
   play therapy as 8–13
social drama, stories as 23
social world, understanding child's 31–6
Song 215–16
space
   for playing 37–9
   therapist–perpetrator compared 66–7
'Spider Man' picture *149*
staring games 42
stories
   definition 22–4
   exceptional–ordinary link 24–9
   narratives compared 29–31
Story of Eric 191–2

Story of the One Eyed Vampire 70–1
Strange Situation 117–19, 120
'Stretch' story 108–9
Sunny the Striker 183–5, *184, 186*
'Super Idiot' story 152–3
symbolism 4, 7

'teddy bear' story 129–30
Teeny-Tiny 208–9
therapist–child
   relationship 3, 8, 11, 78
   'other' role 57
   perpetrator–child compared 66–8
   storyteller role 195–6
therapists
   effect of child's stories on 73–4
   songs and stories for 230–3
There's an Awful Lot of Weirdos in our Neighbourhood 221
Tjihapit 219
toys for play therapy 39, 46–8
Tracy, carer's attitude 32
Transparency of Evil 51
'trapped' theme *123–5, 132–3*
Tricky Pink Power Ranger and the Mermaid 139–40

trust issues 140, 154
'truth' in stories 3, 12, 154

Ubiquitous One 165
unique outcomes 18
Utter Nutters 220

'Vicki' story 162
victimised heroes 167
Victorian Child's Guide to Knowledge 43
Virago Book of Fairy Tales 25

'waiting for a family' story 216–17
Way of a Boy 218–20
We Are All In The Dumps with Jack and Guy 147
We Are All Monsters 72
Wee Bird 26–9
Well at the World's End 215
When A Dinosaur Dad Comes Home From Work 83
Where Did I Come From 81
Why Did The Peacock Scream? 165
Why Gypsies are Scattered about the Earth 212–13
Wicked Knife 6–7
Willy Wonkers 83
wish stories see hero stories
'wonder tales' 195–6
Work for Poets 231

Yellow Emperor 57–8
Yellow Head 87
Yellow Monsters 89
Young Children's Close Relationships 120

'Zarlov' drawing 143

Author Index

Agard, J. 114
Ainsworth, M.D.S. 117, 222
Apuleius 195

Barrie, J.M. 75
Bateson, G. 17, 33, 39
Baudrillard, J. 50, 51, 56, 58, 71, 74, 166
Bloch, E. 167
Bowlby, J. 116–17
Boyden, J. 61
Bronfenbrenner, U. 33–5
Bruner, J. 4, 5, 7, 13, 24

Calvino, I. 196, 231
Carter, A. 25, 201, 208
Clarke–Stewart, K.A. 120
cummings, e.e. 148

Dekker, T. 216
Donovan, J. 19
Dove, R. 115
Doyle, R. 38, 75
Dunn, J. 15–16, 19, 120

Eco, Umberto 1
Engel, S. 77
Epston, D. 17–19

Gergen, K. 13
Giraudy, D. 69

Harris, P.L. 120
Heaney, S. 37
Hendrick, H. 61
Hesse, E. 119
Hillen, E. 218–20
Hunt, R. 195

Inkpen, M. 193

Jacobs, J. 228
James, A. 65
Jenks, C. 61
Joisten, C. 208

Keats, J. 216
Keizer, B. 35
Kitzinger, J. 60

Laing, R.D. 165

Mackay Brown, G. 231
Main, M. 118, 119
Markus, H. 5
Mayle, P. 81
McNaughton, C. 83, 221, 223
Mead, G.H. 14, 57

Namjoshi, S. 53, 54, 74
Neisser, U. 30
Nicholson, B. 11

Nurius, P. 5

Patten, B. 220
Perrault, C. 201, 202–5
Propp, V. 167, 195
Prout, A. 65

Ricoeur, P. 23
Rosaldo, M. 15
Russell, J. 43–4

Sendak, M. 147
Shotter, J. 13, 14
Solomon, J. 118, 119
Stevenson, R. L. 44–5

Teneze, M.L. 167
Thurbur, J. 208
Tizard, B. 120
Tolkien, J.R.R. 166, 167
Turner, V. 23
Tzu, Chiang 166

Umphelby, F. 43

Vygotsky, L. 14, 76

Warner, M. 196, 197
Wells, H.G. 39
Weston, D. 118
White, M. 17–19
Winternitz, M. 165
Work, D. 198

Zipes, J. 196, 201, 205